THINK UNIQUE

Raising a
Successful
Innovative
Child

ORTAL GREEN

Think Unique: Raising a successful, innovative child by Ortal Green
Published by Glittering Minds PTY LTD
PO Box 455, Bentleigh, Victoria 3204

Australia
www.glitteringminds.com.au

Visit the author's website at www.ortalgreen.com

Copyright © 2022 Ortal Green

All rights reserved. No part of this book may be reproduced or transmitted by any person or entity (including Google, Amazon, or similar organisation), in any form or by any means, electronic, including photocopying, recording, scanning, or by any information storage and retrieval system, without prior permission in writing from the publisher.
For permissions, contact: info@glitteringminds.com.au

For information about special discounts for bulk purchases, sales promotions, booking an event, and educational needs, please contact Ortal Green at ortal@glitteringminds.com.au.

While every effort has been made to trace the owners of copyrighted material produced herein, the publisher would like to apologise for any omissions and will be pleased to incorporate missing acknowledgments in any further editions.

First edition published by Glittering Minds 2022

ISBN: 978-0-6452241-2-2 (pbk)

ISBN: 978-0-6452241-3-9 (ebk)

DEDICATION

This book is dedicated to my amazing life partner Robby Green, who supports any adventure I embark upon and my three creative boys, Ethan, Ben and Sean, who taught me the true meaning of being curious, questioning everything, and having crazy ideas.

Contents

Introduction 9

Part 1. Understanding Creativity 19
Chapter 1   What Is Creativity? 21
Chapter 2   Common Misconceptions About Creativity 29

Part 2. Why You Need To Develop Your Creativity 35
Chapter 3   Why Being Creative Is So Desirable 39
Chapter 4   How Being Creative Impacts Your Life And Skills 47
Chapter 5   What Happens To Your Creativity As You Mature? 55

Part 3. The Creative Process 69
Chapter 6   Approach And Mindset 73
Chapter 7   Environment And Wellbeing 99
Chapter 8   The Creative Process 109
Chapter 9   The Creative Process In Action 129

Part 4. Practical Tools And Exercises To Develop Creative Thinking 151
Chapter 10   Imagination 155
Chapter 11   What If…? 165
Chapter 12   What If…? — Repurposing 173
Chapter 13   What If…? — Merging 183
Chapter 14   What If…? — Improving 191
Chapter 15   What If…? — Imagining New Ways 205

Final Note 215
Special People 217
Bonus – More Ideas On How To Develop Your Creativity 219
A Deep Dive Into RIDER 223
Notes 253
A Little Bit About Me… 261

Introduction

It's not easy being a parent. The world has never been more competitive and complex than today. Parents are under pressure to make sure children are academically prepared and have the skills required to thrive in an uncertain future.

Parents have trusted the school system to set up their children for success, in the past. However, parents are realising now that traditional schooling methods are not preparing children for the world of tomorrow, and our children are paying the price.

Our children need to navigate unprecedented change, manage uncertainty, and solve complex problems in our current world. They'll need to be creative thinkers and problem-solvers to thrive. They'll need to become imaginative and resourceful, able to create new solutions to problems we haven't considered yet.

Unfortunately, the vast majority of children are never given the opportunity to develop their natural powers of creativity.

We have a responsibility to make sure that our children have the skills they need to not just survive in this uncertain future, but to succeed and flourish in it.

You want to provide your child with all the opportunities in life. You want to make sure your child develops the thinking and mindset they need to thrive today and in the future. However, it might be challenging to know what you need to do to make it happen.

For this reason, I wrote this book. I wrote Think Unique for parents who want to give their children the best start in life. It is your step-by-step guide on how to raise successful children. Reading Think Unique will inspire you, take you on your own innovative journey and provide you with the knowledge and tools you need to achieve more as a parent.

You are your child's greatest teacher, whether you are home-schooling or not. And I am here to support you on this critical journey.

But before we start, I need to go back a few years to explain how this book came to be.

The journey

I studied computer science and worked in the Hi-Tech industry for many years. While I enjoyed many aspects of computer science, I always felt that something was missing. There was a constant feeling of a void within me. Therefore, I kept searching for more.

As part of my exploration journey to find the missing piece in my life, I studied Design Thinking. I fell in love with Design Thinking right from the get-go. It combines everything I love and enjoy doing. It felt as if I had found what I had been looking for all my life. Right there and then, I knew that this was what I was searching for.

For me, Design Thinking is a way to help others. It is a way to solve problems innovatively while exercising my creative thinking, problem-solving, critical thinking, collaboration, empathy, resilience and communication skills.

Our children need more

Quite quickly, I realised I must teach my children Design Thinking. More than that, I knew I had to teach all children Design Thinking. As a parent yourself, you are probably familiar with this deep desire to provide your child with everything they need to succeed in our world. You might also feel that this is a crucial part of your role.

I have three boys and when they were very young, my focus was on having fun with them and protecting them. As they grew older and entered the education system, I started to look into what my boys needed to thrive in today's world. I looked at the world, at the rapid pace of change driven by technological advancement, and the impact this pace of change brings to the job market.

Today, jobs that have existed for many years are disappearing in front of our eyes, and new jobs pop up every day. Who could have imagined that an e-sport coach would be a profession? Or a drone pilot or a social media manager?

Thriving in today's world is about more than having knowledge. It's about what you do with your knowledge. It is about the mindset you have, your life skills, and the value you bring that computers can't replace.

It's about your superhuman powers. It is about what makes you unique.

It became clear to me that to set children on the path to the best start in life, these children need to develop their unique human traits. To be successful, children today need to develop their creative thinking, problem-solving, curiosity, collaboration, empathy, innovative mindset, critical thinking, and resilience.

Our education system is outdated

Another thing that became clear was the existing gap in our education system. Our education system is built on concepts from the nineteenth century. These concepts are outdated and don't prepare our children for life in the twenty-first century.

I knew I had to do something about it. I knew I needed to build the bridge that provides our children with the skills they need to thrive.

And I knew Design Thinking could be this bridge as this approach to problem-solving develops those unique human traits. I thought to myself that through learning and practising Design Thinking and the creative process, children could develop the skills required to flourish today and in the future. I was eager to test my thinking, so I created a workshop for young children that provides practical hands-on experience in this methodology.

I was happy to see the children's reaction to this workshop. They loved it. They enjoyed learning something new, bringing their creative and authentic thinking to projects, coming up with unique ideas to solve real-world problems, and prototyping their ideas.

After conducting my workshop for a while, the natural next step was to take it to young children in primary schools. I designed a school programme that uses the creative process as the framework for project-based learning and trialled it. Again, it warmed my heart to see the children's positive response to learning and practising in this manner, and how it helps them develop the mindset and skills they need for success. It showed me the natural connection between children and this approach. Because this programme is student-centric, it answers their needs for the freedom to express their unique thinking and ideas and bring these ideas to life.

Design Thinking is the answer

Teachers who adopted this programme told me Design Thinking had transformed them as teachers and their students' way of thinking.

They told me their students became confident problem solvers. They said their students developed their:

- Communication skills
- Collaboration skills
- Problem-solving skills
- Empathy
- Resilience
- Ability to learn and grow from failure
- Confidence in their capabilities

> "The students don't necessarily shy away from a challenge now. They know they can't always know the answer straight away. **They are more comfortable being uncomfortable because they know that they don't always know the answer, but they have to go through a process to find the answer.**
> [Through Design Thinking] they will get even better at problem solving and be more confident to approach problems that they weren't so confident with before.
> Hayden Callahan, teacher and project-based learning leader,
> Edithvale primary school

Research declares Design Thinking as the best way of learning

And today, many research papers support what I have seen for many years on the ground.

These research papers found that children who learn Design Thinking grow to be confident, successful, well-rounded people.

One research done by Concordia University[1] on using Design Thinking in Mathematics concluded that using Design Thinking improves overall results and academic achievements in mathematics. More than that, it concluded that learning in this manner provides children confidence in their capabilities to tackle any mathematical problem.

This research discovered that Design Thinking helps children develop a mindset for success. It allows them to develop a growth mindset and view failure as a way to success. Through Design Thinking, children learnt that they do not have to have the right answer the first time they attempt a solution to a problem. As a result, children developed grit as they tackled problems repeatedly instead of giving up.

This research summarised that learning Design Thinking helps children master literacy, communication, critical thinking, creative thinking, and collaboration skills and develops a mindset for success.

Another research by Hacettepe University[2] also concluded that Design Thinking promotes a higher level of thinking and therefore drives better academic achievements.

This research recommends using Design Thinking to improve mathematics education.

And research by Lesley-Ann Noel and Tsai Lu Liub from North Carolina State University[3] explored whether Design Thinking should be used as the new twenty-first-century education paradigm in primary schools. These researchers found that Design Thinking students develop collaborative problem-solving skills, creative and critical thinking, empathy, social skills, teamwork skills, and a growth mindset. Furthermore, they concluded that Design Thinking challenges students to find solutions to complex problems and supports students' academic performances.

This research affirms that Design Thinking educators can make a lasting impact on students' life skills by teaching them this process.

The research concludes that exposure to Design Thinking education at the primary school level lays a solid foundation that would benefit all children, leading to greater engagement at school and contributing to their future success in their professional lives.

Design Thinking at your home

You might be thinking now – well, this is great. But this is all about schools and teachers, and anyway, my child's school is not a Design Thinking school.

Well, I have a crucial thing to share with you-

You are your child's greatest teacher. Whether you are home schooling or not.

You are the one that develops your child's way of thinking, your child's approach to problems and difficulties. You are your child's most important role model. Therefore, you play a crucial role in your child's education.

Learning Design Thinking changed me as a parent. And I will share with you what I mean by that.

Firstly, it opened my eyes to how I bring my own biases, assumptions and inferences to my parenting style. I suddenly realised that when I am talking with my children, I am not entering these conversations with a mind ready to hear and accept any view, experience and opinion. I noticed that when I am speaking with my children, I sometimes stir the conversation, or word my questions in a leading way. I noticed that my assumptions are interfering with my ability to conduct a proper conversation. My biases and my way of thinking came in the way.

Through Design Thinking, I learnt to start conversations with an open mind. I learnt to leave behind my judgment, assumptions and biases. I learnt to accept and embrace different views. Even if they are opposite to my own. I learnt that there are no right or wrong opinions but different perspectives that depend on other people's gender, upbringing, culture, religion, life experiences, etc.

Due to this shift, the communication with my children became much better. Now I can really explore their thinking and understand where they are coming from. And this understanding allows us to have honest and heart to heart conversations. It brings us closer together as a family.

Secondly, Design Thinking gave me the methodology and tools to help my children develop their high-level thinking. I can now better help them develop their:

- Creative thinking
- Critical thinking
- Empathy
- Resilience
- Approach to failure
- Growth mindset
- Confidence in their capabilities
- Communication skills

In so many different ways.

And you can do it too.

I wrote this book so you and your child can take this journey and enjoy these benefits, too, if you wish to do so.

Think Unique will take you on your creative journey and teach you the creative thinking process, which is the heart of Design Thinking.

You will grow personally, professionally, and as a parent through this journey. Moreover, you will be able to take your child on a fantastic journey to develop their superhuman skills.

It is a path worth taking. It will bring your family closer together and help you create an innovative environment at your home.

How to read this book

I have written this book in a specific order to make sure your journey to develop your creative thinking is an easy one. Therefore, I have divided the book's contents into four parts:

Part One- Understanding Creativity

Part Two - Why You Need to Develop Your Creativity

Part Three – The Creative Process

Part Four - Practical Tools and Exercises to Develop Creative Thinking

It starts in Part One with understanding creativity, including what creativity is, what being creative means, the misconceptions about creativity, and how creativity can be expressed. It is essential first to understand creativity.

The journey then continues in Part Two to explore why you need to develop your creativity, including why being creative is desired by so many people, the impact of being creative on your personal and professional lives, and what happens to your creativity as you mature.

The first two parts are the theory behind this methodology and approach. They explain the what and the why. Understanding this foundation sets you up for a successful journey.

Parts Three and Four contain more of the practical aspects of this journey.

Part Three focuses on developing an innovative environment at your home, from your physical environment to your approach and mindset; then you will learn all about the creative process.

I will walk you through how to use this process to solve problems and provide an example on exploring questions with your child using the creative process.

Part Four provides you with the practical tools and exercises to use, practise, develop your own creative thinking, and help your child develop their own creativity. By the time you reach part four in your journey, you will know that developing creative thinking is the key to success.

Along your journey, if you have any questions related to the content of this book, please don't hesitate to reach out to me at ortal@glitteringminds.com.au. I would like to hear about your experience and your success stories.

A note about the language: This book was written in Australian English, which may use altered spelling or grammar usage from American English. What might appear as a mistake would be correct, as there are many differences.

So, what are you waiting for? Let's start!

PART ONE

UNDERSTANDING CREATIVITY

Like anything else in life, to change and improve something, you must first acquire a deep understanding of the issue or problem.

As a parent, creativity and your creative thinking play a significant role in managing the many demands, which are an integral part of parenting. It impacts your ability to come up with creative solutions on your feet, find different ways to explain a new thing your child needs to learn, solve the many family crises that are part of raising children, and prepare your child for the real world.

Understanding what creativity is, is the first step that sets you on your Think Unique journey.

You might be thinking, *Well, I know what creativity is. Everyone knows what it is. We're not talking about a complex topic here like quantum physics.*

If this is what's going on in your head right now, I completely understand where you are coming from. But this is exactly where you might encounter a big surprise.

Although we grow up with the concept of creativity and use this word frequently, there is quite a gap in understanding what it actually is, how creativity can be expressed, and what we can do to develop our own creativity. This gap in understanding impacts how people perceive their own ability to be creative, how confident people are about their ideas, and whether they think they can become more creative.

Understanding creativity is fundamental to developing your own creativity and creative confidence and developing your child's innovative thinking.

So, let's start by exploring what creativity really is.

CHAPTER 1:
WHAT IS CREATIVITY?

> "The world always seems brighter when you've just made something that wasn't there before."
> —Neil Gaiman, English author

> This chapter focuses on
> - What creativity is
> - What it means to be creative

"Creativity" is a trending word that seems to be everywhere we look—from media articles to job ads, professional and personal courses, and so much more. The word has catapulted into headlines, and I don't think it will disappear from thefront page any time soon.

My purpose is to empower teachers and parents to create tomorrow's innovators and change-makers. To do this, I teach adults and children what creativity actually is and how they can become more creative. I aim to equip every teacher and parent with the knowledge, mindset, and tools to help them and their children thrive today and in the future.

When I teach people about creativity and how to develop their creative thinking through my organisation, Glittering Minds, I hear different opinions about what creativity is. Common answers address the ability to draw well or have different kinds of artistic capabilities. Another strong response is the perception that the "creative" title is out of reach for ordinary people. Rather, it is reserved for the few famous people who impact the entire world with their creativity. The name Steve Jobs is often brought up by participants in my programs, as it has become synonymous with being creative.

But really, what is creativity?

Creativity Defined

Creativity is the ability to come up with unique and valuable solutions for problems.

Let's explore the key components of this definition:

- *Unique* refers to coming up with new ideas with different ways to approach a problem. It is about imagining new ways of doing something that hasn't been done before.
- *Valuable solutions* mean that creativity is not just about coming up with new ideas. Creativity is very much about materialising these new ideas into a solution with value.
- *Problems* in this definition can also be read as *new opportunities*, as in coming up with ideas that solve problems people don't know they have. For example, solving unmet needs or creating a solution for a gap in the market. By doing so, solutions are created to make people's lives easier and more enjoyable.

So, creativity is about finding valuable new solutions for known problems and also about exploring new opportunities.

As a parent to three amazing boys, I want to provide them with what they need to succeed. As an observer of trends in the world, I realised what skills and mindsets children today need to flourish. This created a passion for making it happen and was the driving force for co-founding Glittering Minds. My organisation focuses on empowering teachers and parents by helping them develop the mindset, capabilities, and knowledge they need to create tomorrow's innovators, change-makers and leaders.

One path to realising the purpose of Glittering Minds has been by working with primary school principals, teachers, and students. I believe the earlier we start developing these skills and mindset the better. I have designed a school programme that transforms traditional teaching and learning and prepares the younger generation for the world we live in today and for the unknowns of the future.

There are two layers to our programme. The first layer is transforming teacher's mindset regarding their approach to their teaching and providing them with tools to help them shift to student-centred learning while reducing their work stress and lesson planning time. The second layer is developing children's mindset and skills required for a successful life: problem-solving, creative thinking, collaboration, empathy, resilience, innovative mindset, and critical thinking, to name a few.

When we work with children to develop their creative-thinking skills, we start by asking them: What is creativity?

I love hearing children's different perspectives on this topic. Although I've listened to hundreds of answers to this question by now, I am still amazed by the different answers I get. I want to share with you a beautiful and creative way to explain creativity written by a nine-year-old student: "We think creativity is a space at the back our mind! Past the library and the musical band to a door. A very dull door, but when you open the door, there are colours and thoughts and things you have learned!"

I recommend you ask your child this question. You might be surprised by their answer, and in any case, it will be an opportunity to discuss creativity.

What Does It Mean to Be Creative?

Now that we know what creativity means, it leads us to our next question: *What does it mean to be creative?*

Based on what I see and hear when I help people develop their creativity, it seems that very few people think they are creative. How do you feel about your own creativity? Do you think you are creative? Are you willing to declare in front of your family, friends and colleagues that you are creative?

Very few people will state out loud, with full confidence, "I am creative!" But don't worry if you don't feel very creative yet. I will get you there. I will help you develop your creativity and your creative confidence.

The perception that the title "creative" is reserved for special people is a wrong and damaging perception that puts being creative out of reach for most people. It is far from the reality. Being creative doesn't have to be larger than life. In fact, most often it is not.

Being creative is about improving many little things in your life. It's about finding a creative way to prepare dinner with the limited ingredients you have at home, inventing a new game with your child, or improvising a bed time story as your child is asking for a story they never heard before. It's about making up a silly song about your sibling, coming up with new dance moves in the living room, or coming up with ideas on how to reuse stuff you have at home that you don't want to throw away.

Being creative in your everyday life brings playfulness and fun into your world. It is the special ingredient that brings colour, excitement, good mood, satisfaction, and happiness into your life.

Chapter Summary

- Creativity is the ability to come up with unique and valuable solutions for problems.
- Being creative is about improving little things in your life.
- Being creative is the special ingredient that brings colour, excitement, good mood, satisfaction, and happiness into your life.

Reflective Questions

I am so proud of you for embarking on this wonderful journey, as it will help you better enjoy your life, develop your creative thinking capabilities and give your child the gift of innovative thinking. I can tell you that my creative journey is filled with fun and rewarding experiences. And I am sure you will enjoy this journey too.

Take some time to reflect on the questions below:

1. How do you feel about your own creativity? Do you see yourself as being creative?

   _____

   _____

   _____

2. What are the messages you convey to your child about creativity and what being creative means?

   _____

   _____

   _____

CHAPTER 2:

COMMON MISCONCEPTIONS ABOUT CREATIVITY

> "You can't use up creativity.
> The more you use, the more you have."
> —Maya Angelou, American poet and civil rights activist

> This chapter focuses on
> - The common misconceptions about creativity
> - The differences between artistic and creative abilities
> - Evolving your creative brain

When I talk with people about creativity, I find there are two very common misconceptions that arise. The first is that being creative means being artistic, and second, being creative is a talent we are born with and is fixed at birth.

The First Misconception

Many adults, and children, confuse being creative with the ability to draw well and be artistic. So, if they think they are not good at drawing, if they think they are not really the artistic type, they start to believe they are not creative.

When children start to believe they are not creative, it negatively impacts every aspect of their life. It impacts their learning experience, their ability to be playful and enjoy life, even their self-esteem. They then carry this self-perception into adulthood, where it continues to limit them.

Creativity doesn't mean being artistic. Creativity is an expression of your imaginative mind, and you can express your creativity in many ways. It is important to understand that being artistic and being creative refer to two different abilities: artistic ability and creative ability.

Being artistic is about having a talent in one or more of the categories of art such as the literary arts (e.g., writing poems or stories), visual arts (e.g., painting, drawing, or sculpting), and performing arts (e.g., dancing, acting, or making music).

People with artistic abilities are often born with some talent in art, and then they nurture this talent. But even if you think you weren't born with artistic talent, you can still develop an ability and enjoy expressing yourself in that way. Being artistic involves creativity.

Being creative is about "cognitive creativity," the ability to come up with new ideas to solve problems. It means being able to look at a problem from different perspectives and finding new ways to approach the problem.

We are all born with cognitive creativity, and we can all develop this type of creative thinking. Your cognitive creativity is limitless, and the more you use it, the more creative you become.

It is very important to make the following distinction: being creative is not about having artistic ability. This is an important distinction that all children need to understand. Comprehending this difference means everyone—whether they have artistic talent or not—can believe in their own creativity. It means each child knows they are creative and grows up with creative confidence.

The Second Misconception

The second misconception is the belief we are born with a certain quota of creativity. It is the notion that someone up there provides each newborn with a few sprinkles of creativity, and this is what we get to live with. It is the notion that we can't develop our creativity as it is fixed. You might be thinking you are one of the lucky people who got a large handful of creative sprinkles. Or you might think you only got two or three flakes of it, and there is nothing you can do about it; you just need to accept it.

Luckily, it doesn't work like this.

The brain is an amazing organ. It is not fixed in its capabilities but can reshape itself. It can create new connections to increase its performance in different areas. It can grow and change well into adulthood. This extraordinary ability is called *neuroplasticity*. Neuroplasticity is also the brain's way to repair itself after suffering a brain injury. This means that with consistent practice, you can train your brain to improve existing skills, like creativity, or gain new ones.

Researchers have reported that creativity training can reshape both the function and structure of the brain. The results of one such study showed that training produced significant improvements to the fluency (the number of the ideas) and originality (the uniqueness of the ideas) of generated ideas[1]. These research results revealed that a well-designed training programme is effective in enhancing creativity performance and capabilities.

So, no matter where you are today with your creativity and how creative you think you are, you can develop your creative thinking and creative confidence. You can become more creative, and the beautiful thing is that the more you practise it, the more of it you will have.

Chapter Summary

- Artistic abilities and creative abilities are separate skills.
- You can be super creative while having no artistic abilities.
- You can develop your creative thinking.
- The more you use your creative thinking, the more creative you become.

Reflective Questions

Breaking through the common misconceptions about creativity is an important step on your creative journey. Take some time to reflect on the questions below. It will help you process the new information and recognise what it means for you.

1. What might have changed after reading this chapter in your understanding of creativity and your own creative abilities?

   _____
   _____
   _____

2. How might you help your child have a more truthful understanding of what creativity really is, as distinct from artistic ability?

   _____
   _____
   _____

PART TWO

WHY YOU NEED TO DEVELOP YOUR CREATIVITY

Now that you know what creativity is and that you can become more creative, it's time to look at why you need to develop your creativity. Understanding the why is an important step on your journey to develop your innovative capabilities and create an innovative environment at your home. When you understand the why, it becomes easier to adopt a new approach and mindset.

As a parent, developing your creativity will make a huge impact on your parenting style and the quality of your life. It will enable you to:

- have more empathy,
- welcome different perspectives and opinions,
- enjoy imagining and creating new games with your child,
- have confidence in your ability to tackle any problem,
- become comfortable dealing with problems,
- develop a positive and optimistic view,
- find innovative ways to achieve your goals when facing obstacles,
- enjoy deeper discussion with your child,
- have better relationship with your child,
- prepare your child for success in the real world,
- make a difference and influence people around you.

These are only some of the benefits you will gain from developing your creativity. In the following chapters, you will learn the profound impact of developing this important skill on your life. Now that you know you will benefit greatly from developing your creativity, it is important to note that your child must develop this skill as well. It is crucial for their success in life. I will explain why.

I touched earlier on how different the world we now live in is from the world I grew up in. (And although my boys refer to my childhood as the olden days, it wasn't so long ago!) Huge transformations in such a short time is a trend here to stay. The pace of changes is constantly increasing, and so it's safe to say that the only constant in our lives is rapid change.

To thrive in an ever-changing world, we need to develop the skills to help us adapt quickly and flourish. This is an evolution in action, the survival of the fittest. But these days, it is not about our physical strength anymore. It's about the power of our minds.

So, what has this evolution got to do with creativity? The answer is *everything*, especially in a world where innovation drives so many elements:

- technological advancement
- the pace of change
- the ability to make money
- gaining power (whether it is political, cultural, social, or personal power)
- better quality of life

In today's world, we need to develop an innovative mindset. This is your superpower! But what exactly is an innovative mindset? It is the ability to see new opportunities, have new ideas for improving things around you, and turn constraints into opportunities. It's about imagining a new reality and thinking *What if…?* It's about having no limitations to your thinking, about bringing your unique ideas to life and making them happen.

An innovative mindset is about having a positive impact on your life and the lives of people around you.

Developing an innovative mindset is a necessity. It's not a mindset required only for people who want to be entrepreneurs. We all need this kind of mindset to be successful in our professional and personal life.

What do you need to develop your innovative mindset? What is it that drives this type of thinking and behaviour? You got it right—

it's creative thinking. Taking the *Think Unique* journey will help you develop your innovative mindset and creative thinking.

So, let's take a deeper look into the reasons behind the need to develop creative thinking.

CHAPTER 3:
WHY BEING CREATIVE IS SO DESIRABLE

> "Logic will get you from A to B. Imagination will take you everywhere."
> - Albert Einstein

> This chapter focuses on
> - Why being creative is so important today
> - The future of work and creativity
> - What employers think about creative thinking

When I run my creativity workshops for adults, one of the first questions I ask participants is, "Do you believe you are creative?" Almost all of them are quick to answer with "Not so much." When I then follow up with a question on whether they want to become more creative, there is a resounding "Yes!" from everyone.

Creativity has been a human trait since the dawn of humanity. Remarkable and sometimes very advanced tools testify to human creative genius. These tools originated from different parts of the world and diverse cultures. One example is the boomerang, which was invented as a hunting tool, around 25,000 years ago.

If creativity has existed for so many years, why have we become so fascinated with creativity in recent years?

Creativity rose to stardom on the shooting star that is our modern advancements in technology. It has propelled creativity to the top of our list of coveted skills, and here is why.

Innovation. Creativity drives innovation, and innovation is the driver behind the exponential pace of advancements in technology. To create something new, we need to imagine new ways of doing things. We need to find patterns that no one else is seeing, to merge things that seem unrelated to each other, and to break things down and rearrange the pieces into something different. All of this requires creative thinking. To innovate, we need to be creative.

Automation. Automated technologies, such as machine learning and robotics, are becoming more common in our everyday lives. Machine learning involves computer programs that are "trained" to find patterns in large amounts of existing data and make better decisions and predictions based on new data. The better the machine-learning algorithm, the more accurate the decisions and predictions become as the program "learns" more data. A medical image analysis system that identifies tumours is an example of this.

We use chatbots for customer service needs, facial recognition to unlock our smartphones, GPS to calculate the quickest route to our destination, digital voice assistants like Siri and Alexa to make our lives easier, self-parking cars, and so much more. This automation trend will continue to affect how we perform almost any job, with some jobs more impacted than others. In Amazon warehouses, for instance, there are already more than 100,000 mobile robots working[1], and within the medical field, an algorithm is being used that outperforms doctors in detecting nodules in chest radiographs[2].

As machines in the form of computers with software, algorithms, and applications designed to perform different tasks take over repetitive work, we are luckily left with tasks that require our unique human skills. The automation of mundane tasks frees us to focus on more stimulating tasks, which requires skills machines can't perform—at least not yet.

As you may have guessed already, one of these very special human skills is creative thinking.

The Fourth Industrial Revolution

We are now taking part in the fourth industrial revolution. This revolution is fuelled by innovations based on technologies that drive rapid change, and a broader impact on societies and our lives. Billions of people are connected by mobile devices with extraordinary processing power. Through the internet, access to knowledge is free and unlimited. The use of nanotechnology and biotechnology is transforming the medical field, and around the corner is the use of quantum computing which will enable us to solve even more complex problems—ones that we can't solve with the current technologies.

This revolution will fundamentally change the way we live, work, and connect with each other. Among other things, the fourth industrial revolution impacts the skills we need to have, to succeed in today's world.

The type of jobs available will keep changing, as well as how we perform those jobs. We will increasingly work more closely with machines and use Artificial Intelligence (AI) to support our work. Machines will perform tasks we humans have traditionally done, in some instances replacing the need for humans altogether. This trend clarifies that our unique human traits set us apart from machines and can't be replaced by computers.

You might have heard about attempts to design a creative AI, but I think human creativity can't be replicated with a machine. And I will explain why. Based on machine learning, it might seem as though computers can think creatively and critically. Today, we see that machines are used to make decisions about complex market trading, and machines learn how to diagnose and treat patients. There is even artwork made by a machine, which sold for over 400,000 USD[3].

But are computers creative? To answer this question, we need to look again at what creativity is. Creativity is the ability to come up with unique and valuable solutions to problems. Therefore, looking at AI, we need to explore these questions: Can a machine imagine original ideas to solve problems? Can a machine think critically and decide what a valuable solution is?

To imagine new ideas and be innovative, we need to step away from the known. We need to step away from *what* is and move towards *what might be*. We need to imagine something that doesn't exist.

Can a machine built on algorithms (even when these algorithms are very complex ones) and fed data from what already exists in our world break free from its mechanism and imagine something new? Can a computer really understand the value, beyond numbers and quantified data, that different ideas bring to humans? Can a machine understand the value of joy and laughter?

Yes, AI can easily outperform humans at routine tasks and tasks that require the processing of vast amounts of data. Machine learning is excellent at handling well-defined tasks. However, machines can't imagine. Machines can't understand value, beyond the value you can put numbers on. Machines can't understand the value of emotions. In fact, machines can't understand emotions at all. They can't feel and have empathy for others.

There is a need to define what the meaning of machines' creativity is, as it is very different from the human ability to think creatively.

In the future, we will spend more time in our profession on activities that machines aren't capable of doing, and so we will need to use more social and emotional skills, more imagination and creativity, and more problem-solving and critical-thinking skills.

A 2019 LinkedIn study of the skills companies needed the most found that creativity was the top skill to develop[4]. And according to a PwC (Price Waterhouse Coopers) survey, 77 per cent of CEOs struggle to find the type of creativity and innovative skills they need in their employees [5].

A 2010 IBM study, in which over **fifteen thousand** CEOs from sixty countries and **thirty-three** industries were interviewed, found that creativity was named the most important leadership quality to meet the challenges of increasing complexity and uncertainty in the world.[6]

Creative thinking is the driver behind problem-solving and innovation, which is why it is such a desired skill by employers. Looking to the future, the importance of developing our creative thinking will only continue to rise.

Chapter Summary

- Creativity drives innovation and advancement in technology.
- Machine learning and robotics are becoming more common in our everyday lives.
- The use of AI transforms the job market.
- Unique human traits, like creativity, cannot be performed by machines.
- Employers see creativity as the most important skill they seek in employees.

Reflective Questions

Some people get worried when they learn about the impact of the Fourth Industrial Revolution on our lives and the future of work. Some buy into the "doom and gloom" of machines taking over the world, and humans become redundant. Thankfully, this is far from reality. There is a role and place for each one of us, as each has a unique talent and way to contribute to society. However, we need to be ready for this new reality and develop our unique human skills—those skills machines don't have and can't replace.

Take some time to reflect on the questions below. They will help you understand what the changes in the job market mean for you and what your next steps might be to prepare for the future.

1. What can the use of computers and machine learning mean for my profession?

   _____

   _____

   _____

2. How might I prepare myself for a future where work is increasingly done alongside machines?

   _____

   _____

   _____

3. How might I prepare my child for the future of work?

   _____

   _____

   _____

CHAPTER 4:

HOW BEING CREATIVE IMPACTS YOUR LIFE AND SKILLS

"Creativity is inventing, experimenting, growing, taking risks, breaking rules, making mistakes, and having fun."
- Mary Lou Cook, American actress

> This chapter focuses on
> - The impact of being creative on your professional life
> - How being creative helps you develop other skills
> - The impact of creative thinking on your quality of life

Being able to think creatively impacts every aspect of life. It transforms your thinking, your attitudes and approach, your happiness level, and even your physical health. Developing your creativity is a journey well worth taking.

Let's look at the impact that developing your creativity will have on your professional and personal life, and your overall wellbeing.

Impact On Your Professional Life

Whatever your profession is, it involves the need to solve problems.

In a way, performing our job means moving from one problem to the next one. (You can say the same about being a parent) Therefore, the more creative you become, the easier, less stressful, and more enjoyable your job will be.

You become a better problem-solver. When you develop confidence in your creativity, your approach towards problems changes. Instead of perceiving problems as pain points and obstacles you want to avoid, you see problems as opportunities to practise your creativity. This change in mindset will increase your satisfaction from what you do.

You become an innovator. While your newly acquired attitude makes you a better problem solver, you also enjoy flexibility in your thinking and gain the ability to challenge the status quo. You'll look at how to do things differently, and you'll innovate more at your workplace.

This innovative thinking will positively impact your colleagues' experiences and help with creating a better working environment.

You become more productive. Being creative increases productivity and adds value. For example, that value might mean coming up with ideas on how to perform a task more efficiently, finding simpler ways to get to the needed outcomes, or removing unnecessary steps from processes to save time and effort. By doing so, you create more valuable solutions for your colleagues and clients.

Developing your creativity and applying it at work means you contribute in a more meaningful and unique way.

You increase your value as an employee. As a creative thinker, you will become known as the go-to person when someone has a problem to solve or needs creative ideas. Not only will you help your colleagues, but you will also become a pivotal employee at your work.

Often, the higher your position is in the workplace, the more problems you are expected to solve, and the more complex these problems might be. Therefore, leaders at work are expected to be creative and come up with innovative solutions. Once you develop your creative thinking and demonstrate such abilities at work, you can become a great candidate for promotion.

As you can see now, being creative has many benefits in your professional life and so makes you more employable. Employers are looking for employees who can demonstrate their creative thinking skills. You can add examples to your resume of how you positively impacted your work by being creative in your approach and thinking. At job interviews, you can share stories about using your creativity to solve problems and positively impact the work environment.

Impact On Your Personal Life

The ability to think and solve problems creatively is not only relevant to your professional life but also to your personal life. It will help you solve financial issues or problems within your community. You will find creative solutions to any situation, from everyday problems to broader problems that impact the lives of people close to you.

You have a greater variety of solutions to choose from. Instead of coming at a personal problem with a linear and analytical approach, when thinking creatively, you approach such issues from different angles and perspectives. This gives you many ideas to choose from, and you can select the most suitable solution for the problem at hand.

You gain self-confidence. As you develop your creativity, you build confidence and self-esteem. Being creative comes with the risk of failure—you have to be vulnerable and share your unique ideas and imagination. Therefore, engaging in creative activities boosts your confidence. You come to realise that failure is part of the process, and that's okay. Failure no longer stops you as you either lose the fear of failure or learn to keep going forward, regardless of your fears.

When you have confidence in your creativity, you know you can tackle any problem. You know that even if you don't have the answer now (and often we don't have the answer straight away), you will find it. You trust that you know what to do to get to the right answer. You are not afraid or uncomfortable with sitting with the problem to thoroughly explore it.

You become more resilient. Going through the creative process, you understand that failure is sometimes required to get to the most suitable solution. You know you can learn and grow from failure; you understand what is and is not working, and therefore, you know what your approach should be.

Developing resilience is a gift we can give ourselves and others, as this mindset and skill becomes increasingly important for mental health and the ability to thrive within an ever-changing, fast-paced, complex world.

You increase your ability to focus. As a parent, you may be aware of how children's ability to focus their attention on one single task is declining. The average attention span for the notoriously ill-focused goldfish is nine seconds, but according to a new study from Microsoft Corp[1], people now generally lose concentration after eight seconds! This phenomenon is mainly driven by our busy life and the digital world. Developing creativity increases your ability to focus. You need to be able to focus—to fully be here right now in this moment—to create something meaningful and to truly understand a problem. When you are thinking creatively, everything else disappears. Creativity eliminates distractions by design.

You improve your communication and collaboration skills. Because the creative process includes collaboration, applying creative thinking will help you develop your communication skills. In the creative process, you need to involve other people for their opinions and ideas. You also need to articulate your own ideas and solutions to others to get feedback from them. Working creatively requires you to use verbal and written communication. This means you continuously practise and develop these essential communication skills.

The need to work with others only increases over time; therefore, good communication and collaboration skills will help you thrive.

You naturally become a lifelong learner. Due to the pace of advancements in the world, we constantly need to learn new things and become lifelong learners. Curiosity drives the love of learning and the desire to learn, and the more you develop your creativity, the more curious you become. Your curiosity will lead you along the learning path effortlessly.

You become more adaptable. Developing your creativity also makes you more flexible and adaptable. Your mind knows that nothing is fixed, that everything is moving. You know that the right approach yesterday won't necessarily be the right approach today or tomorrow. As things are moving and shifting, your approach needs to change as well.

Impact On Your Quality of Life

Uncertainty can make people feel uncomfortable, and for some, dealing with uncertainty and unpredictability is a major cause of stress. As you may have experienced, stress can wreak havoc with your mental and physical health. By developing your creativity, you will reduce stress in your life.

You can access a state of flow. When you are being creative, your mind is focused on what you do. When you are focused and fully immersed in an activity, you reach a state of flow. In this flow state, time disappears. Everything else fades away, including your worries, thoughts, stressors, and pain. You are simply in the moment, completely engrossed in your creative activity. Being in this state of flow reduces anxiety and slows your heart rate, helping you to calm down and stay healthier.

Your brain is healthier. When you are engaged in creative activity, your brain is flooded with the feel-good hormone, dopamine. This vital brain chemical makes you feel good about yourself, and so increases your happiness. It gives you energy and motivation, and when you are happier, your immune system is stronger.

You gain meaning and fulfilment in life. Creativity is also a path to authenticity. When you apply creative thinking, you are more connected to your thoughts, feelings, and beliefs. When you are creative, you are true to yourself and give expression to your unique imagination. This leads to a sense of fulfilment and satisfaction, as well as self-realisation. When you are creative, what you do becomes more meaningful and enjoyable.

On top of all the wonderful things I mentioned above, being creative can add playfulness and fun to your life as you better connect with your inner child. And it doesn't stop at only benefiting you. Being more creative benefits the people around you. While you enjoy all these benefits, the people around you also benefit greatly. From work colleagues to friends, and family members, you bring more fun and enjoyment to their lives as well.

Chapter Summary

When developing your creative thinking:

- Solving problems at work creatively and innovatively gets easier.
- You become the go-to person for creative ideas.
- Your enjoyment at work increases.
- You become a more attractive job candidate.
- Your confidence, resilience, adaptability, communication, collaboration, authenticity, and curiosity all get a big boost.
- Your physical and mental health improves.

Reflective Questions

Reflect on the questions below. This will help you understand the impact that developing your creative thinking will have on your life.

1. How do you feel about being a parent? What areas of parenting would you like to improve?

   _____
   _____
   _____

2. Which areas in your professional life might you want to improve?

   _____
   _____
   _____

3. How is your current mental state? Do you need to reduce the stress levels in your life and bring in more fun and enjoyment?

   _____
   _____
   _____

CHAPTER 5:

WHAT HAPPENS TO YOUR CREATIVITY AS YOU MATURE?

> "It is not true that we lose our creative genius when we grow older, but we grow older because we forget to use our creative genius."
> —Debasish Mridha, American physician, philosopher, and author

> This chapter focuses on
> - Why our creativity is declining
> - What type of thinking our society values

All humans are born very creative. This is one of our unique human traits. How lucky are we? However, for most of us, as we grow and mature, something happens that causes our creativity to decline.

NASA wanted to measure their engineers' creativity levels so they could assign their most creative employees to the most challenging projects. Think Apollo 13 with the life-or-death "Houston, we have a problem" situation. The mission control engineers had to quickly come up with creative ideas to solve Apollo 13's major problems from afar with minimal resources.

To accomplish this goal, NASA got in touch with Dr George Land and Beth Jarman to develop a test that would enable them to effectively measure the creative potential of NASA's rocket scientists and engineers[1].

The test proved to be a great success at measuring people's creative thinking capabilities, but the scientists who developed this test were left with a few questions: Where does creativity come from? Are we born with it? Do we learn it?

To answer these questions, they decided to let a group of four-to-five-year-olds undergo the same test they had developed for NASA's adult employees. In 1968, sixteen hundred children sat for this test.

To the testers' surprise, 98 per cent of the children fell in the genius category for imagination. Now the scientists were even more curious to find out what was going on with human creativity. Why did almost all the children test to be creative geniuses? And what happens to their levels of creativity as they grow up? If almost all children are creative geniuses, shouldn't most adults have the same level of creative thinking?

Dr George Land and Beth Jarman decided to turn their research into a longitudinal study and tested the children again when they were ten years old. They found that when the same children completed this test at the age of ten, only 30 per cent fell in the genius category of imagination. In 1983, the researchers again tested the same children at fifteen years old. The downward trend continued, and only 12 per cent of the fifteen-year-olds fell into the genius category of imagination. Later on, when Land and Jarman tested over one million adults (average age of thirty-one), they discovered only 2 per cent of them fell in the genius category of imagination.

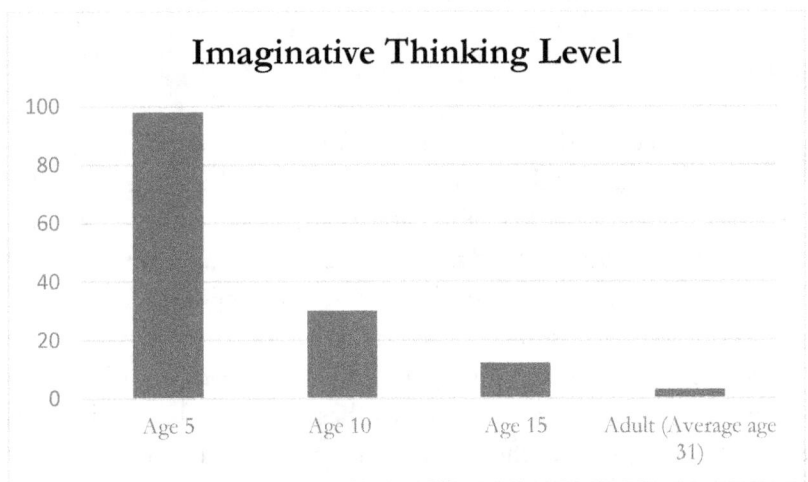

What is going on here? Why do we start our lives as creative geniuses, but by the time we are adults, we are barely creative at all?

I see two main explanations for the decline in our creativity as we grow older: the rise of critical thinking and its impact on our society and school's purpose and design (standardised education). Let's explore each one of them.

Rise of Critical Thinking

"I think therefore I am," the philosopher Renee Descartes said over four centuries ago. We all think. Humans are designed to think. But *how* do we think? When Socrates was thinking about how we think and the quality of our thinking, he concluded that without discipline, our thinking is biased, distorted, limited, misinformed, and uninformed. Since thinking is so crucial to every aspect of our lives, Socrates went on to explore how we can think better and reach excellence in our thoughts. He established the importance of asking meaningful questions to examine our thinking before we accept ideas or information. Socrates recognised the importance of looking into reasoning, challenging assumptions, seeking evidence, analysing concepts, and questioning the reliability of the information. He created a method of questioning known today as *Socratic questioning*, which is an educational method used for what we today call *critical thinking*.

Socrates stressed the need to think systematically, logically, analytically, and rationally, and look well beyond the surface to get to the truth. Scholars across the world started to follow Socrates' method, and during the Renaissance, scholars began to think critically about all aspects of human life, including religion. This trend continued post-Renaissance and opened the door for today's science, democracy, freedom of thought, and human rights. Over the centuries, the concept of evidence-based rational thinking and reasoning became a cornerstone of knowledge in our society. So much so that any type of thinking not currently supported by evidence is tagged as irrational and is at risk for being discarded.

Critical thinking is very important, and everyone should learn how to think critically. But we need another important type of thinking: the opposite of critical thinking. Yes, you guessed correctly again—we need *creative thinking*.

Critical thinking is about being grounded in reality, having evidence, being rational, looking at facts, and getting to the bottom of what exists, of "what is". In contrast, creative thinking is about breaking away from "what is" and imagining new realities, new possibilities, things that don't exist, and things that might seem far-fetched or ridiculous. It is about coming up with new ideas without evaluating them. It is about letting your imagination take you to places that don't yet exist. Here is an example: not far back, a surgeon and a patient had to be in the same room for the surgeon to operate on the patient. This was how it was always done. At some point, someone came up with the idea of remote surgery, of having a surgeon operating on a patient when the surgeon is not at the same location as the patient. This idea might have sounded crazy and not grounded in reality when people applied critical thinking and evaluated this idea. However, this far-fetched idea became the new reality!

You will read more about why critical thinking and creative thinking are opposite types of thinking in Chapter 6: Approach and Mindset. In this chapter, I talk about nine key approaches to life, and approach number six is about the need to separate critical and creative thinking.

As a society, we value rational thinking over creative thinking, which is a shame as the two don't contradict each other; rather, they complement one another.

Putting critical thinking on a pedestal means it receives a lot of love and attention while creative thinking gets pushed aside, too often perceived as a less important kind of thinking.

Both types of thinking are equally important, and therefore, the same importance should be placed on developing critical and creative thinking in children.

Purpose and Design of Schools

What is the purpose of schools? Why do they exist? (By "schools," I am referring to the compulsory education system we have today.) When I explored these questions, some of the information I found was disturbing. Let's look together at a brief history of schooling.

The first version of school is thought to have been created in Egypt around 2,060 B.C. This was a school for elite boys. Only the royals, rich people, and specific professionals' sons attended schools at that time.

In China, around 1,600-B.C., government schools were formed for the elite, and private schools were formed for the common people. (This is exactly the opposite of what is happening with public and private education today.)

In Greece, around 500-B.C., anyone could open a school and decide on its curriculum. Parents could choose a school based on its curriculum and fees. Receiving education was a common thing for boys, and even poor families sent their sons to school. In these diverse schools, students could learn gymnastics, art, performing arts, history, literacy, rhetoric, math, politics, logic, natural history, and more. Apart from the fact that girls weren't included in this educational system, it seems awesome to have had a system that encouraged diversity in schools. As each child is unique, and one size doesn't fit all, it's wonderful to have schools with that much curriculum variety.

Fast forward to Medieval times in Europe around the fifth to late fifteenth century, when the Catholic Church was in control and feudalism was the structure of society. During these times, monks, priests, and bishops took ownership of teaching, and the educational system became strictly religious. The Church used education to control people, capitalising on the lack of education available to lower classes and girls.

The use of education for power, control, and political gain didn't end with Medieval times. About 1760 in Europe and the US, the Industrial Revolution required people to transition from working on the land to working in factories. The economic success of countries was dependent on having a productive and obedient workforce in their factories.

Horace Mann was an American politician and educational reformer. In the early nineteenth century, he pushed for free, standardised, compulsory education for each child. Mann believed that a common learning experience would "equalise the conditions of men." He also believed that schools should prepare children for future employment (at the factories) by instilling values such as obedience to authority, discipline, promptness in attendance, and organising the time according to a ringing bell.

Mann argued that universal public education was the best way to turn unruly American children into disciplined, conforming citizens, and he won widespread approval for implementing this public school system. Mann's system eventually spread to the rest of the world and is the foundation for today's universal school system.

You might be thinking, *But that was many years ago, surely the current schooling system has come a long way since then. Surely today's schools are different?* Sad to say, schools today are still about punctuality (adhering to the ringing bell), being obedient, and not questioning the status quo. More than that, the education system is standardised. Every student is expected to learn, be measured against the same standards, and fit into the mould.

If you are an employee, or have been an employee, you know that your employer sets *key performance indicators* (KPI) by which each employee is measured. Each employee knows their KPIs and spends time and effort to meet them. After all, this is what your employer wants you to achieve, and it impacts your employment, career progression, and compensation. As an employee, you won't focus your efforts on things outside your KPIs. In fact, most people won't spend time and energy at all on things outside their KPIs.

Schools are measured as well. Principals, teachers, and schools have KPIs. And whilst your own KPI rating, as an employee, stays private and confidential to you alone, a school's rating is published for everyone to see. The school's rating impacts how parents perceive the school, and therefore, the enrolment rate of the school, the principal and teachers' careers, and how many teachers will compete for a job at a specific school, which might have an impact on the quality of the teachers at that school. This puts a lot of pressure on school principals and teachers. As if this is not enough, countries are measured against each other's educational system. And the pressure continues to rise…

So, what is actually being measured? On a country level, I'll use Australia as an example. In Australia, students are tested on their knowledge in literacy and numeracy. Every so often, they are also tested on their knowledge in science, civics and citizenship, and information and communication technology. This answer-driven assessment is called NAPLAN.

This means that teachers must focus their efforts on making the students practise for the NAPLAN tests, in place of everything else.

The students are asked to memorise many things and go through a series of mock tests. This is done at the cost of spending time on meaningful learning in the classroom. Students are expected to know how to answer questions instead of asking questions to explore the world around them. Schools become answer-driven systems, not question-driven systems, and are guided by the results of assessment tests. One outcome is many students become disengaged, and they miss out on learning what's important for their well-being and success in life.

Looking from an international perspective, countries compete over which country's children are best at memorising material using the international student assessment called PISA. Inevitably, students and teachers must spend more time practising how to answer different types of numerical questions.

It's easy to measure the ability to spell and solve numerical questions; it's much harder to measure creative thinking, collaboration, empathy, curiosity, resilience, questioning skills, happiness, and well-being.

It's time for governments to wake up and think about what children today need to become well-rounded, successful adults. Is it spelling long, difficult words? Or is it creative thinking, entrepreneurship, and resilience? What is important for the success and future of countries: children who can memorise dates of historical events or children who are curious and self-learners?

What You Measure Becomes What You Teach and Where You Focus All Your Efforts.

Impact of Standardised Testing on Creative Thinking

Professor Yong Zhao works at the School of Education at the University of Kansas and is a professor in Educational Leadership at the Melbourne Graduate School of Education in Australia. He performed a research on the relationship between the rank countries received on the Programme for International Student Assessment (PISA) versus how well these countries perform in innovation.(Based on The Global Entrepreneurship Monitor report[2]. The Global Entrepreneurship Monitor, or GEM, is an annual assessment of entrepreneurial activities in more than fifty countries. GEM monitoring started about the same time as PISA assessment. GEM is the world's largest entrepreneurship study.)

Professor Zhao found a significant negative relationship between PISA performance and indicators of entrepreneurship. Countries with higher PISA scores have fewer people confident in their entrepreneurial capabilities.

Professor Zhao's research has shown that creative entrepreneurship and test-driven curriculum standardisation are contradictory to each other. Standardised testing rewards the ability to find the "correct answer" and therefore discourages creativity, which drives innovation.

Coming back to Dr George Land and Beth Jarman and their research, they concluded that non-creative behaviour is learnt. This means creativity is unlearnt at schools. The way our education system is designed is causing a decline in our creative thinking.

We need to make sure our education system encourages children to think in new and unique ways. The educational system needs to move away from focusing on one "right" answer and standardised testing. The type of thinking and behaviours suppressed by our education system are required for the development of creative thinking and our ability to come up with innovative solutions to the problems of the modern world.

The Influence of Parents and Teachers

There are two other important topics regarding what influences children's creativity that I want to address. The first is that teachers and the education system are not the same things. The second is regarding how children are nurtured within their immediate family.

Addressing my point about teachers, I want to stress that we need to separate the system from the teachers who operate within it. Most teachers are not involved in policymaking or curriculum design, and they might not be aware of the impact of the education system on their student's creative thinking capabilities.

During the years I've worked alongside teachers, I've gained a great appreciation for what teachers do and the many pressures they are under. Many see the flaws and problems within the education system and know that this system needs to change. Some do what they can to drive change within their classroom or school, but making changes within the entire system is complex and hard. I believe that many teachers know what needs to change and why it needs to change. The difficult part is how to go about it.

Although Dr George Land and Beth Jarman concluded that creativity is unlearnt at school, it is important to note a forgotten factor impacting creativity. That is whether creative thinking is being developed and nurtured within the immediate family. This is where you, as a parent, can make a huge difference. You can develop your child's creativity and make sure your child stays the creative genius they were born. And I will show you how to do so.

Chapter Summary

- All humans are born super creative.
- Our society values facts, evidence, and rational thinking more than creative thinking.
- Schools are designed to create obedient citizens.
- Schools are driven by measuring students' ability to memorise information and answer numerical questions.
- Creative thinking is unlearnt at school.
- Parents and teachers can develop children's creative thinking.

Reflective Questions

You can become a creative genius, and you have the power to develop your child's creative genius. Take some time to reflect on the following questions:

1. Think about your interactions with your child. In these engagements, what value do you place on rational thinking? What value do you place on creative thinking?

   _____

   _____

   _____

2. When you provide your child with a problem to solve, how do you guide them? Do you expect them to come up with a specific solution? Do you ask them to look at the problem from different perspectives and come up with more than one solution? Are you expecting them to come up with one "right" answer to this problem?

   _____

   _____

   _____

3. What is your current approach to your child coming up with questions? Are you encouraging them to come up with questions on any topic?

_____
_____
_____

PART THREE

THE CREATIVE PROCESS

This part is all about the creative process: creating an environment that nurtures creativity, what the creative process is, how to help your child learn in a more meaningful and impactful way, and how to use the creative process as a framework to do projects with your child.

To learn something new is to be curious about it. Curiosity is firstly about a mindset and approach to life. The true meaning of curiosity is being open to possibilities, being comfortable with uncertainty, and adaptable and flexible with your thinking. This is required as you know the starting point of your exploration journey, but you don't know where this journey will take you.

It is about really listening to diverse opinions, ideas, and experiences different from your own and leveraging this diversity to see things differently, change your perspective, and learn from it. It is about being open-minded.

This is what creative thinking and the creative process are all about. You are taking this journey and developing your own creative thinking to support your child in adopting this mindset and learning these skills too.

We all know that if we want to develop our muscles, we need to exercise them regularly. If you're going to see results, it will require you to change your habits, have self-discipline, and be consistent about it. Developing your creative thinking works in the same way. To develop your creativity, you need to exercise your creative and imaginative thinking.

As per NASA's research on creativity, most of us are 96 per cent less creative than we were as children. But the great news is you can reverse it and get back to 98 per cent creative geniuses.

The first step is to adopt the approaches and mindset I will share in Chapter 6 and then learn how to create an innovative culture and environment in Chapter 7.

In Chapter 8, you will learn the creative process, which is the framework to facilitate your child's learning. Chapter 9 provides you with an example on how to use the creative process as a framework to explore questions with your child. You will learn how to create unique and innovative learning experiences at your home.

When you get to Part Four, you and your child will be ready to further exercise your creative muscles with the practical tools and activities I will provide.

The creative thinking process is your generic framework to help your child develop unique thinking capabilities. You will be able to adapt the difficulty level of each step to your child's abilities.

It is also up to you to decide how much technology you want to include when using this framework. You can facilitate such learning without any use of technology if that suits your needs and circumstances.

All you need to do now is keep an open mind and continue your exciting and rewarding journey to think unique.

Icons and Emojis

There are a few icons throughout the text of the book to make it easier to spot specific parts:

Tips for how to implement the *Think Unique* approach.

Weight-lifting emojis mark an exercise. There are three levels of difficulty. When you see one emoji lifting weights, this is an entry-level exercise— anyone can do it.

 Two weight-lifting emojis indicate the exercise is a bit more advanced. Young children starting their creative-thinking journey might need to wait until they progress further along the journey. If you want to check whether your child can tackle this level, let them try it out and gauge how they cope with it.

 Three weight-lifting emojis indicate the exercise is much more advanced.

These exercises are more appropriate for teenagers and adults due to the complexity of the thinking involved. However, for certain gifted younger children, these exercises will be a good way to stretch their thinking skills.

CHAPTER 6:

APPROACH AND MINDSET

> "If you find a path with no obstacles, it probably doesn't lead anywhere."
> —Frank A. Clark, American lawyer and politician

> This chapter focuses on
> - Nine key approaches to life that give you the right mindset
> - The mindset required to drive your success and creative thinking
> - How to develop approaches for creativity and success

I've found that the keys to success and transformation lie within one's *mindset*—a set of assumptions, methods, or notions held by a person arising out of their worldview and belief system.

Even if you were born with special talents, received an elite education, and grew up in a wealthy family, you need to approach life with the right mindset to succeed—whatever success means for you!

And if you didn't grow up within these wonderful conditions, don't worry. With the right mindset and attitude, you can aim for the stars and reach them.

Let's look at nine key approaches to life that you can adopt to give you the right mindset for living a successful, creative life.

1. Drop perfectionism
2. Embrace failure
3. See an obstacle as an opportunity
4. Keep an open mind
5. Get comfortable with being uncomfortable
6. Separate critical and creative thinking
7. Have a bias for action
8. Be optimistic and keep going
9. Develop creative confidence

Learning and practising the creative thinking process (see Chapters 8 and 9) will help you and your child adopt these nine key approaches to life.

1. Drop perfectionism

> "At its root, perfectionism isn't really about a deep love of being meticulous. It's about fear. Fear of making a mistake. Fear of disappointing others. Fear of failure. Fear of success."
> —Michael Law, American author

If you are driven by perfectionism, now is the time for you to drop it. Being creative is about letting go of the notion of perfect. It's about knowing that there is no such thing as perfect. Perfect doesn't exist, it's an illusion. What does exist is a constant improvement loop, learning and reiterating.

Being creative is about knowing that everything is in a state of improvement (including ourselves) and that nothing and no one will ever get to a fixed state of "perfect," so save yourself the pain of trying to get to a non-existent place.

How Can You Go About Dropping Perfectionism?

- Practise self-empathy and forgive yourself.
- Be mindful of your self-talk. Whenever you recognise negative self-talk, change it to a positive version.
- Look at the big picture and focus on the important parts.
- Calibrate your standards. Getting a task done is more important than trying to make it perfect.
- Give yourself permission to do a quick "first draft" which can be improved later.
- Seek feedback, as it helps you improve.

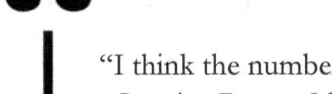

"I think the number one thing it [The Creative Process] helped me with is providing the students with more opportunities to get feedback on their work. They constantly revising their work and trying to improve their ideas."
—Hayden Callahan, project-based inquiry leader, Edithvale primary school

> "It [The Creative Process] helps them in getting better at getting feedback and understanding what good feedback is. It helps them not to be attached to their ideas, look at things from different perspectives, and choose the best idea." — Amy Cain, year 4 teacher, Edithvale primary school

2. Embrace failure

> **"To live a creative life, we must lose our fear of being wrong."**
> —Joseph Chilton Pearce, American author

The biggest obstacle to being creative (and to living an authentic life) is fear of failure.

Fear of being wrong, fear of being vulnerable and exposed to criticism, and the fear of being perceived as stupid. It is this fear that so often paralyses us.

Being creative requires you to be vulnerable. To open and share your ideas, which may still be in their infant state, with others. To share ideas that haven't been developed and potentially need a lot of work to become great.

Unfortunately for all of us, our society still doesn't value failure. There has been some shift in recent years, but we are still not there. Not only is failure undervalued and perceived as being an impediment to success, but within our society, we do our best to avoid failure. It is not recognised as a precursor for success.

In reality, failure leads us to success. When we fail, we are "failing forward" to success. This is what Sir Altitude, the amazing Michael

Jordan, has to say about failure (as quoted in a Nike YouTube commercial), "I have missed more than 9,000 shots in my career. I have lost almost 300 games. On 26 occasions, I have been entrusted to take the game's winning shot, and I missed. I have failed over and over and over again in my life. And that is why I succeed."

Being wrong can be very useful. It's one of the best ways to learn what's working and what's not working. Getting it wrong also helps you stumble upon unexpected discoveries. It can lead you in some fascinating directions that you wouldn't have discovered otherwise.

I think we need to stop using the word "failure" due to the negative connotation people associate with it and start calling such events "learning experiences." At the end of the day, this is what failure is. Perhaps changing the terminology will help people feel more comfortable with the concept.

Putting your creativity forward for everyone to see can be scary. You might feel very vulnerable. You are putting yourself out there—your thoughts, your ideas, your creativity—for everyone to judge. But you need to separate the criticism of your ideas from your self-worth. You need to understand and embrace the fact that not everyone will think the same as you. And this is okay. This is actually a good thing because diverse thinking helps you get to better ideas and better outcomes. If all of us thought the same and had the same ideas, the world would be a very boring place, and there would be little room left for innovation.

Another thing you need to remember is that even when other people don't think your idea will work or is a good idea, it doesn't mean you need to accept their thinking as the "right" way. Great ideas often get rejected and receive negative criticism from other people.

This is best illustrated by a story about a single mum. This woman lived in a small flat, was unemployed, and was living off government welfare. But she had an idea and a dream. She was dreaming a story, a story she wanted to share with the rest of the world.

This woman spent many hours at coffee shops, writing her book while her daughter slept next to her in a pram. Life wasn't easy for her. She suffered from severe depression and had suicidal thoughts. It took her six years to write her book from her imagination, and when it was finally ready, after many years of hardship, she sent it to a publisher. The publisher sent her a rejection letter. But it didn't stop her. She sent her book to more publishers. Over the course of a year, she sent her book to twelve different publishers. One after another, they all rejected it.

But this woman wasn't going to give up. She believed in her dream and her story. "I wasn't going to give up until every single publisher turned me down, but I often feared that would happen," she was later quoted as saying.

So, she kept going, believing in her idea and creativity. Eventually, the book captured the attention of the Bloomsbury Publishing house and was published in 1997. The title of the book is *Harry Potter and the Philosopher's Stone,* and it was written by the now very famous author, J.K. Rowling. At the time of writing this book, *Harry Potter and the Philosopher's Stone* was ranked as the second-most-sold book in the world, with 120 million copies sold[1].

J.K. Rowling continued to write six more books in the Harry Potter series. All of them are at the top of the list of the most sold books in the world. Furthermore, the Harry Potter books were turned into blockbuster movies and inspired a successful theme park.

As a result of believing in herself, her creativity, and her idea, about fifteen years after starting to write the first Harry Potter book, J.K. Rowling went from being a single mom on welfare to a successful billionaire author. (She later donated a large portion of her money to charities and therefore dropped off the billionaire's list.)

The message here is don't be deterred by rejection. If you believe in your idea, go for it. Don't give up. Receiving criticism of your ideas doesn't mean that you are not creative or that your ideas don't have value. It doesn't mean anything about you as a person. After all, with creativity, there is no wrong or right idea. Some ideas will be less suitable as solutions or won't be "liked" by others, but it doesn't mean they are wrong. Sometimes it means there is a better idea or a better solution for the problem at hand. Sometimes it's just a matter of timing. The timing might not be right for a specific idea, but a few years later, when things change, the same idea that was rejected before might flourish.

I know it is difficult to do so, but you need to separate how well others accept your ideas and thoughts from your own self-worth. You create many ideas and thoughts over the course of your life, and a single idea doesn't define you. It is not who you are. A single idea or thought is only a small part of what your creative thinking can produce. A rejected idea doesn't reflect on your capabilities, your creativity, or who you are.

I believe that most of us got scarred during our childhood. Most of us received negative feedback about our creativity when we were young, which has negatively impacted our confidence in our capabilities.

Maybe when you were young, a relative or a friend made a negative comment about your ideas: "This is the most stupid idea I have heard!" Or maybe someone commented on something you made: "This looks so ugly…" Or maybe as an adult, you put your ideas forward at work, and a colleague said, "This is ridiculous, it will never work." And so you lost confidence in your unique ideas and ability to create, and you decided to leave it for others to do.

When I run sessions with children on problem-solving, I often see this fear of failure. It's always sad for me to see it in children as young as eight. When I work with children, I ask them to work on real-world problems to solve. At some point, the children are asked to come up with ideas for a solution. There is no judgment, and everyone is encouraged to come up with as many crazy ideas as they can. But there are always those children who don't want to share their ideas.

These children are afraid to share their ideas as they might not be the "right" ideas. These children are already so afraid of being wrong, that they prefer not to take part at all.

How Can You Go About Embracing Failure?

- Tell yourself that a failure is a beginning, not an end.
- Know your failure gets you closer to success.
- See failure as a great learning opportunity.
- See failure as a way to get mentally stronger and resilient.
- Know that any successful person failed many times.
- Know that not being afraid to fail enables you to chase your dreams and to live your life to its fullest.

> "[As a result of learning The Creative Process] students think more deeply about it. You talked at the start about falling in love with the problem, not the solution. It gives them permission to fail and trial, to fail and trial until they narrow it down. And they understand what they want to achieve from it."
> —James Whitla, principal at Edithvale primary school

3. See an obstacle as an opportunity

> "...the imagination is unleashed by constraints. You break out of the box by stepping into shackles."
> —Jonah Lehrer, American author

Almost no one looks forward to encountering obstacles. I believe no one gets excited when life suddenly throws a constraint onto your path. Usually, the first reaction is one of annoyance, and if it is a big obstacle, you might also feel like a victim. You might think, *Why is this happening to me?*

But life is great at continuing to throw these kinds of surprises at you, and most often you don't have control over external events. Therefore, you need to choose between one of these two mindsets:

1. Obstacles prevent me from achieving what I want.
2. Obstacles open new possibilities.

I think it's safe to assume you should choose the second option.

The next time you encounter an obstacle, know that you can control how you react to it. Know that there is a way forward. Know that you can transform this constraint into an opportunity. You are not a victim of the circumstances. You create your own path.

When it comes to creative thinking, an obstacle is an opportunity to be creative. This is your chance to imagine new ways of doing things. This is your chance to break free from "path dependence" (the tendency to think in a fixed way based on decisions you've already made) and create an exciting new path.

An obstacle can be a blessing in disguise. You might be stuck in a rut without even realising it, and this constraint will push you to make a change. An obstacle can lead you to new adventures, new people, and wonderful, new experiences.

You might end up very far from where you started, and possibly, in places you never imagined you'd be.

How Can You Go About Seeing Obstacles As Opportunities?

- Know that you are not a victim of external circumstances.
- Trust you can transform any obstacle into a great opportunity.
- Know that you create your own path.
- Know that an obstacle can propel you towards your goals.

4. Keep an open mind

> "The only way to discover the limits of the possible is to go beyond them into the impossible."
> —Sir Arthur Charles Clarke, English writer

An important part of the creative process is letting go of your assumptions and looking at things and problems around you with fresh, beginner's eyes. These are the eyes of a child who hasn't yet learnt why things are done in a specific way and why they can't work in a different way. A mind without habitual thinking, a mind that has no limitation on its thinking.

Creativity is a matter of having an awareness of your own beliefs, biases, and assumptions, being aware of the limitations of your own thinking, and then working to remove those limitations. Letting go of them so you can see things in a neutral way. Letting go of them so you are only limited by your own imagination. Losing the judgment. Getting rid of the notion of right and wrong.

When I say there are no wrong ideas, I'm not referring to dangerous ideas which, for example, ignore human rights. Such ideas are immoral and wrong. What I am talking about here is the tendency to see your own ideas, perceptions, and beliefs as the "right" ones and other people's different perceptions, ideas, and beliefs as "wrong."

Remove thinking along the lines of *can* or *can't* work, *stupid* or *smart* idea. This will enable you to see so many new possibilities, to see diverse perspectives.

Any idea, any different way of seeing things can lead you to exciting new realities, new solutions, that you never thought of or imagined before. Think about the amazing things that are part of your everyday life—you don't even question them.

For example, aeroplanes. A flying machine that carries people up in the air. Isn't this amazing? Doesn't it sound like the most ridiculous and crazy idea?

When the Wright brothers were working on the creation of a flying machine, most people called them crazy. Most people thought it would be impossible to do. Most people thought they would never succeed. But the Wright brothers kept an open mind and didn't put boundaries on their thinking. They went ahead with their crazy idea until they succeeded.

Can you imagine the world without aeroplanes?

Keeping an open mind opens doors to amazing experiences and enables you to be more creative in your thinking.

How Can You Keep An Open Mind?

- Lose judgment. There is no right and wrong, only different perspectives.
- Be mindful of your assumptions and biases and put them aside.
- Remember that today's crazy idea could be tomorrow's reality.

> "Prior [To learning The Creative Process], the students were coming up with great ideas, but their ideas were based on what they wanted and not considering the needs of the people they were designing these solutions for. The biggest change is in how they are able to consider multiple perspectives regarding an issue or a challenge and tackle it from different angles, and they aren't just considering what they want to do."
> —Hayden Callahan, project- based inquiry leader, Edithvale primary school

5. Get comfortable with being uncomfortable

> "The creative person is willing to live with ambiguity. He [or she] doesn't need problems solved immediately and can afford to wait for the right ideas."
> —Abe Tannenbaum, educator at Columbia University

Our society and culture rush to solutions. When people face a problem, they immediately jump into solution mode. Quick! We must solve this problem now!

There are two main reasons why humans find it difficult to stay with a problem and instead rush to a solution. The first is they are uncomfortable with ambiguity, and the second is they think that not knowing is a sign of weakness.

Feeling uncomfortable with ambiguity. Staying with a problem for a long time makes people uncomfortable. We dislike the feeling of being in a state of ambiguity, and this discomfort often leads to us taking one of two approaches:

1. Hiding the problem under the carpet, just ignoring it, and hoping it will miraculously go away. This often feeds the problem, which then gets bigger and bigger until the problem is too big to ignore, or it has exploded and created more damage.
2. Rushing into the first solution that comes to mind without exploring what the real problem is, what its root cause is, and what the right solution is. The outcome of such a rushed approach can make it an even longer-term pain when the original problem comes back like a boomerang because the wrong problem was solved, or the root cause was never resolved.

Either way, people often don't spend enough time understanding the problem.

Not knowing is seen as a sign of weakness. Many people are under the impression that others expect them to know all the answers right away, and they put this unrealistic pressure on themselves. But when you rush to get rid of a problem, you miss an opportunity to gain an understanding of the situation and its root cause. You miss the opportunity to explore whether what you perceive as the problem is really the problem and whether there are other related problems you need to look at.

When you stay with the problem and endure the ambiguity for longer, you open yourself to many possibilities. It can help you get to the bottom of the problem and come up with the most suitable solution.

You need to become comfortable with being uncomfortable. You might think now, *What is that again? This sounds weird! How can I feel comfortable with being uncomfortable?* I know it sounds a bit strange. What I mean though is to get comfortable with uncertainty and with not knowing. To get comfortable with saying to others, *I don't know the answer yet*, while trusting that you can find the answer later and feeling okay (not weak) with not knowing for now.

To be able to get to the real root cause of a problem, as opposed to what might lie on the surface, you need to feel comfortable staying with a problem for a longer period of time. You need to pause and not rush to find a solution. You need to get to know the problem inside out and upside down. You need to look the problem in the eye and not blink first.

How Can You Get Comfortable With Being Uncomfortable?

- Know that you don't have all the answers while feeling confident about your ability to find an answer.
- Get comfortable with replying to others with *I don't know the answer yet.*
- Know that enduring a state of ambiguity can bring better outcomes.
- Know that taking the time to solve a problem reduces the chance of it coming back to you.

"[As a result of learning The Creative Process] the students don't necessarily shy away from a challenge now. They know they can't always know the answer straight away. They are more comfortable being uncomfortable because they know that they don't always know the answer, but they have to go through a process to find the answer."
—Hayden Callahan, project-based inquiry leader, Edithvale primary school

6. Separate critical and creative thinking

> "The chief enemy of creativity is good sense."
> —Pablo Picasso

As discussed in Chapter 5, you need to use two equally important types of thinking throughout your life: critical thinking and creative thinking. Each one of these types of thinking serves a different need.

Critical thinking (also known as "convergent thinking") is about applying logic, refining, narrowing down, and evaluating options; in short, analysing and criticising.

Creative thinking (also known as "divergent thinking") is about having no boundaries, imagining different futures, thinking *What if...?*, exploring possibilities, and generating unique and crazy ideas.

As you can see, these two types of thinking are very different from each other. They require different kinds of brainpower, and different types of brain activity.

As children in school, or as adults in our workplace, we are often expected to apply both types of thinking at the same time. But when you are asked to come up with new ideas and simultaneously expected to evaluate them, your brain won't be able to do so—at least, not in an effective way since boundaries required by critical thinking cripple creative thinking. Creative thinking doesn't need to abide by any rules. It doesn't need to be explained by current knowledge. It doesn't need to be logical or make sense.

Children and adults need to learn to separate these types of thinking, to be able to defer judgment when coming up with new ideas. Then, after finishing the creative thinking process, they can apply critical thinking to their new ideas.

To unleash creative thinking, the boundaries need to be removed. Creative thinking requires dreaming. Dreaming of new ways to do things, dreaming of futures that don't exist yet. You need to go past the known, the safe, the feasible, and logical. You need to leave critical thinking behind.

The relationship between critical thinking and creative thinking is like the relationship between a car's gas and brake pedals. Thinking creatively is like pressing on the gas pedal: the harder you press, the faster you go, and the more ideas you have.

When you apply critical thinking, you are assessing and narrowing down options. You investigate what is possible and what is not, what is logical (as per what society defines as logical) and what's not. You are pressing on the brake pedal. You stop dreaming. You are very focused and grounded in your thinking.

When people are asked to apply critical and creative thinking at the same time, the brain can't handle it. To continue the metaphor, it is the same as trying to drive a car while pressing on the brake and the gas pedals simultaneously and wondering why the car is not moving.

How Can You Go About Separating Critical and Creative Thinking?

- Define what type of thinking is required for each task you perform. All tasks should fit into one of these two buckets: Creative thinking or critical thinking. A task can only fit into one bucket.
- When working with your child:
  - Clearly define what kind of thinking is expected from them to complete a specific task.
  - Set the ground rules for creative-thinking tasks. (See Chapter 7: Environment and Wellbeing for guidance in creating a safe environment.)

- Make sure you and your child adhere to the ground rules.

> "It [The Creative Process] is something where your creativity can burst out of your head."
> —Year 5 student
>
> "It is really fun; I enjoy thinking in a different way and the creative aspect."—Year 4 student
>
> "I think it is fun and helps you be creative in your own way!" —Year 6 student

7. Have a bias for action

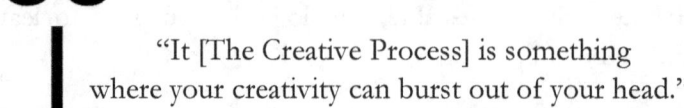
"Knowing is not enough; we must apply. Being willing is not enough; we must do."
—Leonardo da Vinci

Creativity and imagination go hand in hand, but they are not the same thing.

Imagination enables you to create mental representations of things that may not exist in your past or present environment or may be impossible or unreal. It is the ability to produce something intangible in your mind. Imagination is a powerful capability of different cognitive processes—planning the future, reliving the past, feeling empathy, or creating art.

Creativity is using imagination to generate new ideas which are then used to create something of value. The difference between imagination and creativity lies within the action, within the creation itself. Creativity comes from the Latin word "creo," which means *to create, to make*. It's about bringing your ideas to life, about producing something tangible. It's about *doing*.

A bias for action means you don't need to have a full plan upfront to start creating something. It means you are not afraid to act even though you are not sure where you're going. It means starting to take steps that will help you figure out things and get a better understanding of where you need to go even before you've figured everything out. It means taking action to help you learn and move forward.

Having a bias for action means your default approach is to do something, no matter how big or small. It's the mindset that the right time to start is now.

How Can You Go About Having a Bias for Action?

- Act when faced with uncertainty. Your actions will help you figure it out.
- There is no magical "perfect moment" to start. The time to start is now.
- If it's too big, break it down, and start by taking smaller steps.
- Don't let planning come in the way of doing.
- Trust that you will figure it out as you go.
- When you have a choice between action and inaction, choose action.

> "I like how we get to build things and present them." —Year 4 student

> "It is really fun because we get to create stuff and solve problems, and I love working with my friends."
> —Year 3 student

8. Be optimistic and keep going

> "Our greatest weakness lies in giving up. The most certain way to succeed is always to try just one more time."
> —Thomas Edison

We all feel at times like we've just hit a wall. It is natural to get frustrated and feel you've had enough. Sometimes, you need to act on these feelings. For example, let's say you decided you want to learn how to play the guitar. You participated in many lessons but struggle with learning this skill. You feel frustrated and think it might not be the right thing for you. In this case, it might be time for you to let go and move on.

There are times when you might take an idea forward and work hard on making it happen, but at some point, understand it's not the right way to go. You might realise that you need to move on to the next idea. This is not giving up. This is following a path, reaching a dead end, and changing course. It's not giving up because it gets too difficult.

But at other times, when faced with setbacks, when you need to deal with problems left, right, and centre, when things simply don't work for you, you might want to give up. At these times, you need to take a break, re-group, keep an optimistic view, and keep going.

Anything worthwhile I've done in my life was difficult. Any meaningful experience in my life came with many challenges. If I were to give up when it got difficult, I would have missed out on everything in my life that was worth living for, everything that I am proud of.

During a discussion with another author recently, he told me it took him thirty years to become an overnight success. Success takes time and perseverance. Success requires grit. It requires you to keep going, especially when the going gets tough.

When you are doing something big and meaningful for yourself, things may get difficult. It's not going to be a walk in the park. But you are strong. Probably stronger than you think. And those setbacks are there for you to learn from and grow. All those difficulties and frustrations will eventually be worthwhile. Knowing that you faced obstacles, kept your optimistic view, and overcame those obstacles is a great feeling. Knowing all that is also a great confidence-booster.

So, believe in yourself. Once you put your mind to it, you can do anything.

How Can You Go About Being Optimistic and Keeping going?

- Know that nothing can stop you but yourself.
- Help is always there. You just need to ask for it.
- Trust that beyond these obstacles and setbacks lies success.
- Look after your mental health and do what helps you recharge.
- See obstacles as what is getting you closer to where you want to be.

> "It [The Creative Process] gives them [the teachers] permission to challenge the kids a bit more and dig deeper; it sets up a safe environment. They are happy to challenge the students to think again; the right answer isn't always the first one. That rolls through to other parts of their teaching as well, English and maths: how can you do that a bit differently, what is the next step for that, how can you tweak that, improve that, it is probably a better mindset for [the teachers] as well"
> —James Whitla, principal at Edithvale primary school

9. Develop creative confidence

> **"The worst enemy to creativity is self-doubt."**
> —Sylvia Plath, American poet

Creative confidence is having the belief in your ability to create something of value and drive a positive impact in the world around you. Creative confidence is something you can develop. It comes from the experiences you have, your mindset, and your approach.

I want you to know that you are creative. You have great ideas and a great imagination. And I will help you develop it further. The more you practise your creativity, the more confident you will become.

Creative ideas come in all shapes and sizes. You might come up with a creative idea as to what kind of business your child can start or how to go about marketing the product your child wants to sell. You might come up with a creative idea on how to reduce the level of CO_2 in the air and prevent global warming.

The ideas you come up with every day to help solve small problems in your daily life and the ideas that change the lives of everyone on this planet are all a result of creative thinking.

Don't fall into the trap of believing that creative ideas must be jaw-dropping. Don't put creativity out of your reach by thinking that the title "creative" is only for extraordinary people who put a dent in the universe.

Don't compare yourself to others. Focus on being creative in your own unique way. You are special. There is no one else like you.

Having creative confidence is about being willing to be wrong: willing to fail, learn from it, and try again. It is about knowing that you will get to the right solution, no matter how many times you need to try different things. By developing your creative confidence, you will gain another benefit. Becoming confident in one area of your life impacts your confidence in other areas, so by developing your creative confidence, you will boost your overall confidence.

How Can You Go About Developing Creative Confidence?

- Creativity is a choice. Choose to become more creative every day.
- You are creative. Don't let the voice in your head tell you otherwise.
- View failure as a learning opportunity.
- Seek new learning experiences. You will gain knowledge and get comfortable with uncertainty.
- Learn from experts. This knowledge will give you confidence in your decisions.
- Get used to questioning everything. It will uncover gaps and drive your decision-making confidence.
- Imagine different perspectives to think differently.

> "Another part to the impact [of The Creative Process], is the research and the feedback in real-time; there is a practical component to it as well. Rather than thinking they [the students] have the answer, they know they got the answer. The difference between thinking and knowing is huge."
> —James Whitla, principal at Edithvale primary school

People often wonder why they don't reach their goals. It's easier to look for an external reason rather than looking within. But the reality is the biggest obstacle in your way to success, is you. This is a good thing, as you can remove this obstacle by changing your mindset. And you can start doing so right now.

Chapter Summary

- Success in life is all about having the right mindset.
- By adopting nine key approaches to life, you will be able to reach your goals.
- These nine key approaches will boost your creative thinking and your confidence.

Reflective Questions

To kick off your transformation and begin cultivating a successful mindset, take some time to reflect on the questions below.

1. Look at each one of the nine key approaches mentioned in this chapter. Which ones do you need to develop? (You might already master some of them.)

   _____
   _____
   _____

2. What will you do to develop these approaches? What will you change to cultivate these approaches? (Think practically what it means to your everyday life. Make a plan on how you will develop these approaches.)

   _____
   _____
   _____

3. How might you help your child develop these nine key approaches for success in life?

   _____
   _____
   _____

CHAPTER 7:

ENVIRONMENT AND WELLBEING

> "You can't just give someone a creativity injection. You have to create an environment for curiosity and a way to encourage people and get the best out of them."
> —Sir Ken Robinson, British author, speaker, and international advisor on education

> This chapter focuses on
> - Looking after your brain
> - Your physical environment
> - Your social/cultural environment

Your environment (what you see, what you eat, how you talk to yourself and others, how other people are talking to you), your physical condition, and your mental wellbeing all play a role in you being able to reach your full creative potential.

There is much you can do to create the conditions you need for developing your creative thinking so your creativity can flourish. Let's start with your mental and physical wellbeing and unpack what we know about your most amazing body part: your brain.

Your Brain, Creativity, and Stress

Scientists used to think the brain mostly develops during infancy, and at some point, when you reach adulthood, the brain stops developing. Then, once you hit midlife, your brain starts to decline. It's quite a relief to know that this is not how the brain works.

The brain is constantly changing and developing. At no point in your life is your brain "fixed." And as we age, some cognitive functions of the brain are improving. A Seattle Longitudinal Study that tracked the cognitive abilities of thousands of adults over fifty showed people actually performed better on tests of verbal ability, spatial reasoning, math, and abstract reasoning in middle age than they did when they were young adults[1]. (This is great news if you are middle-aged!)

As the brain grows older, some connections in the brain are strengthened. These types of connections are the ones that increase your creativity by enabling you to recognise patterns faster and better find connections between things that seem unrelated. This helps you make better judgments, see the big picture more easily, and understand the overall implications of specific actions, ideas, and changes. Overall, these connections improve your ability to come up with unique ideas to solve problems. Perhaps this is why we have the saying, "older and wiser"[2].

Scientists studying the brain discovered that moments of creativity take place when the mind is calm and relaxed[3]. Therefore, your stress level directly impacts your creativity, and it makes sense to reduce stress in your life to be more creative. While this is often easier said than done, trust me, it will benefit all aspects of your life.

But not all kinds of stress are the same. There are both the "good" and the "bad" kind, each having a distinct impact on your body and brain.

The human body is designed to experience stress as stress is a survival mechanism. The "fight or flight" stress response is something that has helped humans survive for many years. Therefore, stress is certainly an important part of our lives, and it is natural to experience stress. But we need to distinguish between "good" stress and "bad" stress.

"Good" stress is the type of stress that helps you become more focused on what you do and helps you to perform better. An example is when you feel stressed over an assignment you need to submit, and you focus your energy on working on this task, doing it to the best of your ability. Or, when you feel stressed sitting for an exam, the stress helps you focus on the exam's questions to perform better.

"Bad" stress is the type of stress that lingers in your life, chronically interfering with your ability to live your life to the fullest. Chronic stress can also have a negative impact on your brain. It can change the brain's structure, kill brain cells, shrink the brain, and negatively impact your memory. To sum it up, chronic stress compromises the brain's cognitive abilities[4].

In addition to reducing "bad" stress, you also need to feed your brain with the nutrients it needs. A well-balanced, healthy diet can provide your brain with what it needs. Your brain is a sophisticated and complex organ that requires a lot of energy. In a resting state, it consumes about 20 per cent of all the energy your body needs[5]!

Exercising regularly will also help your creativity as physical activity releases the brain chemical serotonin, which calms your mind. Physical activity can also protect your brain from a decline in learning and memory capabilities. It also improves the brain's neuroplasticity, which is the brain's ability to form new nerve cells and create new connections between neurons [6].

Environments That Stimulate Creativity

Surrounding yourself with the right environment will help stimulate creative thought and collaboration. This "right environment" has two components: the physical environment and the social/cultural environment.

Physical environment. Your physical environment can trigger thoughts and feelings, both positive and negative ones. For your environment to positively impact your creative thinking, it needs to make you feel relaxed, comfortable, and appropriately stimulated.

You perceive your environment with all your senses; therefore, environments designed to stimulate creativity need to cater to your different senses. Such environments will include visual aspects, as well as sounds you hear, the space and objects your body senses, and what you smell.

Regarding your visual environment, some colours can help you relax and generate more ideas. Green and blue, for example, are considered to be colours that enhance creative performance.[7] Colourful spaces can help people lose their inhibitions and feel more childlike, playful, and adventurous.

There are studies about the effect of light on people's state of mind. Natural light, for example, is known to increase happiness and wellbeing. Natural light contains "blue light" which increases the levels of dopamine, your "feel good" hormone, and lowers levels of cortisol, your "fight or flight" hormone. This means that being in an environment lit by natural light can make you feel more relaxed and happier.[8]

In terms of your sense of hearing, the sounds around you can have an impact on your mindset, emotions, and creativity. Some people find it difficult to work with noise around them, while others think better when there is background noise. For others, music helps them think.

Other factors to consider in your environment include the temperature, and the type of furniture you have in your living or working space. For example, having an informal seating arrangement, such as beanbags and sofas, can help you to relax and be better able to generate ideas. The amount of empty space in an area can allow you to move freely—a benefit for kinetic thinkers, those who think better when they move. All of these can have an impact on your creativity.

In terms of your sense of smell, I believe you already know how certain smells impact you. This might range from a stinky smell, which prevents you from being able to concentrate on anything else, to a strong chocolatey smell that distracts you by making you hungry for a candy bar. A pleasant background fragrance from incense or an aromatherapy diffuser can make you feel relaxed and more able to concentrate.

Everything you sense in your environment has an impact on your creative thinking. As each human being is unique, you need to find what works best for you. To create an environment with optimal conditions for a diverse group of people (like your family members), you will need to cater, as much as you can, to different styles and needs. To make sure everyone is engaged and comfortable within this environment, you will also need to consider different thinking styles like auditory, visual, and kinetic.

Social/cultural environment. There is much more to an environment than its physical properties. A significant factor in how we feel is the social and cultural aspects of an environment. (Some call it the "energy" in the room.) In the same way that your culture influences what you wear, how you talk, and what you eat, your culture also drives your creative thinking capabilities.

Being creative and expressing creative ideas can be scary. It requires you to open up and be vulnerable. So, whether it is at home, at work, or in the classroom, the right environment to encourage creativity is one where you feel safe—safe to voice your opinions and safe to fail.

A social environment that encourages creativity needs to provide you with the freedom to think uniquely. With the freedom to explore. With the freedom to be different. Such an environment needs to be supportive, and that means trusting the people around you, feeling comfortable being true to yourself, feeling you can be authentic, and bringing out the "real" you. You need to know, without any doubt, that your ideas will be respected, no matter how crazy they might sound.

New ideas are fragile, and your creative confidence can be fragile too. The key thing here is to create an environment where everyone feels safe enough to bring forward their ideas. Everyone should know they are not going to be judged or criticised for expressing their unique thinking. It's necessary to nurture an environment of courage and empathy if creative thinking is going to develop and flourish.

Creativity thrives where people work together, and so social and cultural environments should encourage people to learn from each other, share, and collaborate. This is the fertile ground on which innovation can take root and grow.

Millions of species live on planet earth, but only one of them landed on the moon, created supercomputers, and dominated the planet. All of this was achieved thanks to the ability of humans to imagine, create, and innovate.

Did you know that some animals are quite creative too? Researchers have realised that humans don't have a monopoly on creativity. Animals invent new behaviours, use tools in different ways, and design innovative methods that provide value and solve problems. Primates with big brains, like apes for example, are using tools extensively and exhibiting great cognition and learning capabilities [9].

If animals are capable of creative thinking, then why haven't they invented the smartphone? It turns out that it is not enough to be creative. To reach the level of human inventiveness, a species needs to have a culture of sharing information and knowledge and building on each other's ideas.

When a member of a species can share information accurately, other members of this species can replicate that information and build on it. And soon enough, the accumulation of small innovative ideas leads to the amazing things that humans have been able to create.

Therefore, a culture of innovation means a culture of sharing information and knowledge, and of building on each other's ideas.

You can use the below points as agreed upon protocol in your family to help create a safe, creative environment. (You can download it from https://www.glitteringminds.com.au/resources.)

- There are no silly ideas.
- While coming up with ideas, don't evaluate them.
- The more ideas the better.
- Crazy ideas are awesome!
- Build on other people's ideas.

Chapter Summary

- Exercising reduces stress and increases your creativity.
- Your physical environment plays an important role in your ability to think creatively.
- When designing an environment that fosters creativity, consider all your senses.
- The social and cultural environment has a huge impact on creative thinking.
- Cultivate a culture of trust, support, empathy, courage, inclusion, collaboration, and sharing.

Reflective Questions

You can create an optimal environment for creativity and nurture your creative machine, your brain. Take some time to reflect on the following questions:

1. How might the current design/setup of the physical environments you live and operate in support your creative thinking? (Think: your home, work environment etc.)

   _____
   _____
   _____

2. What might you change in the current design/setup of the physical environments you live and operate in, to better support your creative thinking?

   _____
   _____
   _____

3. How might the social/cultural environments you live and operate in support your creative thinking?

   _____
   _____
   _____

4. What might you change in the social/cultural environments you live and operate in, to better support your creative thinking?

   _____

   _____

   _____

5. How might you design both a physical and a social/cultural environment to cultivate creative thinking in your child?

   _____

   _____

   _____

CHAPTER 8:

THE CREATIVE PROCESS

"Creativity is not an escape from disciplined thinking. It is an escape with disciplined thinking."
-Jerry Hirschberg, American automotive/industrial designer

> This chapter focuses on
> - What the creative process is
> - How to use the creative process

When we think of inventors and innovators and their creative processes, we often picture in our heads the lone person who suddenly has a *Eureka!* moment to come up with a unique idea. You may be familiar with the story about Isaac Newton sitting under an apple tree. When an apple fell on his head, Newton came up with an idea he formulated into his famous Law of Gravity. Or the story about Archimedes who took a bath and figured out how to precisely calculate volume and density while enjoying sitting in the warm water.

These are the stories we grew up with, the "light bulb moment" stories of lone geniuses who suddenly came up with amazing theories, new and unique understandings of how our world works, all on their own. They all had a *Eureka!* moment.

We love these stories about great minds who stumble onto something new and innovative without any hard work. It's like listening to a fairy tale, and who doesn't like a good fairy tale? But the truth is that innovation and coming up with new ideas is never a single event. Rather, it is a long process. Even though these moments of inspiration and epiphany happen suddenly, they are the result of a lot of hard work done by many people. Much knowledge that already existed had to be studied, ideas from other people understood, experimentation done, as well as many failures happened, and much time passed in contemplation.

New ideas don't come out of nothing. All new ideas lean heavily on what is already known and on other peoples' ideas and theories. Instead of occurring as sudden moments, new ideas are the result of what we can formulate in something called the *creative process*.

In this chapter, I will take you on a tour of the creative process, unpacking the five steps of the creative thinking process. If you are home schooling or want to explore questions with your child at home, this process is the framework you will use to plan and design such learning. In the next chapter, I will show you in greater detail how you can implement this process at home through a real-life example and step-by-step directions.

The starting point of the creative process is opening your mind to a wide range of information, knowledge, and ideas from many diverse areas. Although the question or challenge you'll work on with your child relates to a specific topic, you should explore both knowledge and ideas on this topic and branch out to other areas. You might be thinking, *Why do I need to explore other topics not related to the problem I need to solve?* If so, I'm glad you asked.

You might have heard of *cross-pollination* and *self-pollination* processes in nature. Cross-pollination is the process of sharing pollen between different plants. Self-pollination is the process of transferring pollen within a flower or between flowers of the same plant. Both these processes are used in nature to create the plant's seeds and ensure its continuity.

When comparing the two processes, there are clearly evolutionary advantages for cross-pollination. The seeds created by cross-pollination are more genetically varied, more adaptable to changes in the environment, and more resistant to diseases. Cross-pollination usually produces more and better-quality seeds.

Your ability to come up with diverse ideas works in the same way. If you "cross-pollinate" your brain with information from different fields, on various topics, then your brain will be able to create more unique ideas, and these ideas will be of better quality.

One example is how the architect Mick Pearce came up with new ideas on how to design big buildings that are environmentally friendly and energy-efficient. Around 1990, Mr Pearce was assigned the task to design a 350,000 square-foot building of office space and shops in Zimbabwe. Around that time, Mr Pearce watched a nature show on termites. He was impressed to learn about climate control within termites' mounds. Despite the outside temperature fluctuation from 40 degrees Celsius to less than 0 degrees Celsius, the termite mound's temperature was stable at around 30 degrees Celsius.

Mr Pearce was curious to learn more about how termites build their homes and how this can be used to design buildings that use less energy. After researching this topic, he applied this new knowledge to his designs. The building Mr Pearce designed in Zimbabwe uses 90 per cent less energy than its neighbour buildings while keeping a comfortable temperature.

The Five Stages of the Creative Process

The process of creative thinking—of what needs to happen for you to explore a problem, a challenge or a question and come up with new ideas—can be divided into five stages. But while you can follow these steps to becoming a more creative thinker, the process is not linear. You may return to any of the five steps at any point in the process, if you wish. And to make the steps easier to remember, think of yourself as a traveller along on the journey, using the acronym

RIDER (**R**esearch, **I**ncubate, **D**ream, **E**valuate, and **R**ealise) to capture the five stages of the creative process.

- Step 1. **R**esearch
- Step 2. **I**ncubate
- Step 3. **D**ream
- Step 4. **E**valuate
- Step 5. **R**ealise

Let's look closer at what is entailed in each one of these steps.

Step 1. Research.

At the research stage of the creative process, your brain is opening up and acting as a sponge to absorb significant amounts of information. During this stage, you should be exposing yourself to diverse perspectives. You could be talking with people from diverse walks of life who work in various professions, opening your mind to diverse information, ideas, and thoughts. (I know I am using the word "diverse" a lot here, but diversity is *the* key here!) This is the material your brain will be able to work with later on when it needs to create new connections and come up with new ideas.

You'll want to research how similar questions or problems are solved in entirely different fields. Get inspiration from other industries' approaches to similar pain points or goals.

You can also look for inspiration in science fiction books, TV series, and movies. You might be raising an eyebrow now, thinking, *How can fiction stories help me during the research phase?* If like me, you grew up watching Star Trek on TV, you know that many futuristic inventions and technologies used in the show have become a reality. For example, the iPad, flip phones, Bluetooth headsets, Siri, flat-screen TVs, and Google glasses were all futuristic inventions used in *Star Trek*.

Exploring science fiction in all its forms can reframe your perspective on the world and inspire you to think and imagine new ways of doing things. It frees your thinking from your current knowledge, assumptions, and false constraints. It's so effective in freeing the imagination that sci-fi writers are being hired by think tanks, politicians, and corporations to imagine what the future of technological innovation and social phenomena might look like.

 A big part of this research stage is about exposing your child to people from different occupations, cultures, religions, countries, and upbringing.

It's about developing their understanding that there is not just one truth. The way you see things depends on so many different factors. There is no one "correct" perception of an issue. Different people will have different perspectives, and all these perspectives are valid. (You and your child can explore different points of view online. You can read articles written by different people or watch interviews with diverse people to get exposure to multiple perspectives.)

> "My students have changed their approach to problem-solving. When thinking of a solution to any problem they got, even a disagreement in the yard playing with somebody, they are now more likely to consider how other people involved might be feeling, rather than just themselves and how it affects them. I think they are starting to change their mindset from just thinking about themselves to thinking about what other people want and need."
> —Amy Cain, year 4 teacher at Edithvale primary school

Step 2. Incubate.

At this stage, your subconscious mind processes all the information absorbed during the research stage and connects it to the problem, the challenge, or the question that occupy your mind. This is where your conscious mind needs to let go of constantly thinking about what you are trying to solve. Instead, get busy with unrelated tasks that relax you and don't require much brainpower—like Isaac Newton relaxing under a tree or Archimedes taking a warm bath.

This is when you go for a walk and enjoy nature or play basketball, soccer, or whatever game you enjoy playing with your friends. This is when you take a relaxing bath or shower, or maybe you just sing and dance. Simply do whatever activity relaxes you and doesn't require deep thinking. While you are having fun, your subconscious mind will be busy processing information and creating new and interesting connections that can help solve the problem you are working on.

You need to trust this part of the creative process and know that the answer will come to you when you let go of pursuing it. When you stop being obsessed with it and clear your mind, ideas will start to surface. They will bubble up in your mind, as if from out of the blue. Just make sure you capture these ideas before they disappear. Ideas and thoughts are like butterflies; they suddenly appear and are quickly gone, so write them down in a notebook.

 To prepare your child for the incubation phase, give them time to contemplate the question they are working on and the information they gathered.

To do so, you can ask them about what they have learnt. These questions can be:

- What did you learn?
- What might surprise you? Why?
- What do you want to learn more about?

- What was the most important thing you have leant? Why?
- How can you apply the things you have leant to solving our question?

By providing your child with prompting questions, their brain will think about the challenge or question they are working on and continue to do so when doing relaxing activities at home. Once your child has had enough time to think about the problem, they will be able to move to the next phase.

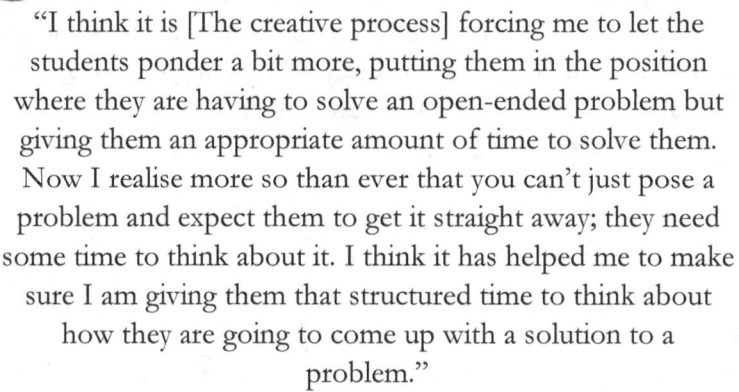

"I think it is [The creative process] forcing me to let the students ponder a bit more, putting them in the position where they are having to solve an open-ended problem but giving them an appropriate amount of time to solve them. Now I realise more so than ever that you can't just pose a problem and expect them to get it straight away; they need some time to think about it. I think it has helped me to make sure I am giving them that structured time to think about how they are going to come up with a solution to a problem."
—Hayden Callahan, project-based inquiry leader at Edithvale

As preparation for the next stage, *Dreaming*, you can frame the question you are working on. When you frame the problem, you get a clear picture of what you want to achieve and who are you designing for – who your target audience is. It will help to write down your answers to the items below:

1. Problem statement: state the question you are working on.
2. Who is your target audience? Who is involved in this question? Who will be impacted by a solution for this question?
3. What are your target audience's needs and difficulties?

Your responses should be at the forefront of your mind when you *Dream* ideas and, later on, when you *Evaluate* those ideas. Your ideas need to solve a problem for your audience, to be solutions your target audience needs and wants to use. Your ideas need to be of value to others.

Step 3. Dream.

At this stage in the creative process, your subconscious mind is coming up with ideas, insights, and new connections. Thoughts will suddenly appear in your conscious mind as if coming from nowhere. This is a result of exploring and learning different things and taking the time for incubation. You feel like you're having *Eureka!* moments, "light bulb moments." It's a very exciting stage, sometimes referred to as *brainstorming*.

As I mentioned before, thoughts tend to disappear quickly; therefore, make sure you capture all your thoughts. Don't judge or evaluate these thoughts and ideas. Resist the urge to immediately assess the feasibility and logic behind your ideas. We are trained to instantly evaluate our ideas and thoughts and apply critical thinking, but at this stage, simply write them all down. In brainstorming, you are going for quantity; therefore, the more ideas, the better.

Work with these thoughts, build on them, and come up with more ideas. Don't be afraid to come up with crazy and irrational ideas. Don't put any limitations on your thinking. Just flow with it, have fun with it, and write down all your ideas.

You can start the process of coming up with ideas without waiting for ideas to spontaneously bubble up in your mind. You can start brainstorming ideas after gaining a deep understanding of the problem you are working on and after you have framed it. Starting to imagine different solutions will kick off this *Dream* stage and help to stimulate your brain to think of new connections and new ways of thinking. Even after you finish brainstorming, your subconscious mind will continue thinking about the problem in the background.

You might find that suddenly, when you least expect it, more ideas appear in your mind.

It's important to know that when brainstorming, the first ideas that come to you are the trivial ones, the ideas that are within easy reach for your brain. (The brain tends to be lazy, but this is a whole other story in itself!) Let those initial ideas out, all the not-so-exciting and unexceptional ones; then, at some point, you'll get stuck. You'll think, *That's all folks. I can't come up with any more ideas. This is all I have.* When you get to this stage, which we all do, you need to push beyond it. You need to find something that will get you over this hurdle because beyond it lies your most unique and innovative ideas. If you manage to get over this flat line, you'll find treasures.

You might be wondering now, *How can I get beyond this point?* Often, it's by thinking about or hearing really crazy ideas from other people. One of the tricks I use to get past this point is to think about crazy ideas that people will be shocked by.

For example, let's say I'm working on this question: How might we reduce traffic congestion in Melbourne's city centre? Some crazy ideas can be:

1. People must use a zip line to get in and out of the city.
2. Confiscate any vehicle that enters Melbourne's city centre.
3. Arrest any driver of a private vehicle who enters Melbourne's city centre.

When you saw my crazy ideas, you might have thought to yourself, *These aren't just crazy ideas, they're terrible ideas!* and you might be right. Maybe some of them are bad ideas, but at this stage, when we are coming up with ideas, it's important to defer judgment and go for quantity. The more ideas the better. There are no bad ideas.

Then, once I write down all my crazy ideas, I look at them and build upon them to create more ideas. I look at the essence of these crazy ideas and find the seed I can build on.

For example, when looking at the idea of confiscating cars, the essence is taking the cars elsewhere. Building on this concept, we can create a place outside the city centre, where people will need to park their cars and use public transport to get to the city.

You can spend some time now reflecting on my crazy ideas and see how you might build on them. What kind of unique ideas can you generate?

Another way is to turn everything upside down to trigger new thinking and ideas. Looking at one of my crazy ideas, "Arrest any driver of a private vehicle who enters Melbourne's city centre," let's flip the concept of punishing drivers for entering the city on its head. Instead of punishing them, let's reward them. What if we pay such drivers a sum of money for each day they don't enter the city with their car? What if we provide them with public transport for free? What if we provide them with a big chunk of money if they don't enter the city with their car for a whole year?

You might want to reflect on turning the concept of my other two crazy ideas upside down.

It makes a massive difference to brainstorm ideas with a diverse group of people, as each one brings their unique perspective and thinking to the task. This means that together, by building on each other's ideas, wonderful new ideas are generated.

Brainstorming. There are a few basic guidelines for brainstorming. (You can download these rules here: https://www.glitteringminds.com.au/resources

1. There are no silly ideas. (Defer judgment)
2. While coming up with ideas, don't evaluate them (Whether it's your ideas or someone else's ideas).
3. The more ideas the better. (You will have more ideas to choose from.)
4. Crazy ideas are awesome. (They help you look at a problem from new angles.)

5. Build on other people's ideas. (It generates better ideas.)

Brainstorming At Home

Brainstorming is a wonderful way to develop different solutions to problems as a family. You can also use brainstorming to come up with many ideas for your next holiday or for anything else you would like to plan as a family.

Here is how you can go about it:

1. Gather your family.
2. Set a fun and playful mood, as being in a fun mood increases creativity.
3. Go over the brainstorming guidelines. (You need to make sure everyone follows the guidelines, especially deferring judgment on ideas)
4. Supply many Post-it notes and pens.
5. Write the challenge question on a big paper and place it where everyone can see it.
6. Ask all family members to write their ideas on Post-it notes. (One idea per Post-it note)
7. Once everyone has finished coming up with ideas – ask each one to read aloud their ideas and to stick the Post-it notes with their ideas in a place where everyone can see them.
8. Ask all family members to build upon the ideas they have heard from everyone and write more ideas on Post-it notes.
9. Aim to have between thirty to fifty ideas.
10. Once you have finished coming up with ideas, group similar ideas together.

 When facilitating a brainstorming session with your child or as a whole family, do your best to create a safe environment where everyone feels comfortable sharing their ideas.

I find that when working with children, some don't feel comfortable sharing their ideas with others. Two common reasons for this are:

- A child might be harsh on their own thinking. They might apply judgment on their own ideas and think their ideas are stupid.
- A child might be a perfectionist, being unsure about having the "right" idea and therefore refusing to share it.

Help your child understand there are no silly or stupid ideas and no "right" or "wrong" ideas. All ideas are valid and welcomed.

Step 4. Evaluate.

Now that you have many ideas to work with, it is time for the next stage: evaluate them. When evaluating ideas, it is helpful to have the framed question or problem in front of you.

Start by grouping similar ideas. This helps reduce the number of ideas you now need to evaluate.

Next, consider what the most important or influential factors are for a successful solution. Use those factors as the criteria for this step.

You'll want to create simple criteria that will enable you and your child to evaluate the ideas and decide which to take forward. It is best to have a maximum of five criteria.

The criteria can be driven by budget, timeline (how long will it take to implement this idea?), complexity to implement (for example, if technology is required to implement this idea, does that technology exist?), and feasibility (can we do it?), etc.

Have a discussion with your child regarding which criteria you should be using to evaluate the ideas. Let them come up with ideas and explain the reason behind them. It can be a good exercise in verbal persuasion. Ask your child to explain why the criteria they came up with should be used. These criteria should be relevant to the question or problem you are working on.

You can use a scale of zero to five and score each idea based on how well it performs against each one of the criteria, where zero is not meeting the criterion and five is fully meeting the criterion. When you perform this exercise, see if the ideas that scored low can be modified to get a higher score. (You want to give each idea a fair chance as you don't want to miss good solutions and too quickly reject ideas that might have great potential.)

If you want to take forward four ideas, pick the four with the highest score.

Now that you finished the Evaluation step, you've reached the exciting stage of taking your top-ranking ideas forward and making them real.

> "It [The creative thinking process] helps get our students to think more critically about the way that they are approaching problems. Previously we may have sent students to come up with their ideas for solutions for problems without considering the people they are designing the solutions for. This journey has been helpful; they are now really conscious of who they are designing for, and they are using the information they gathered to better form solutions for these problems."
> —Hayden Callahan, project- based inquiry leader at Edithvale primary school

Step 5. Realise.

For an idea to become valuable, you need to make it real. This is the time to bring one or two ideas to life and test them with your target audience.

Create a quick, inexpensive, and *rough* prototype for the ideas you decided to take forward at the end of the *Evaluation* stage. (A *prototype* is not intended to look and feel like the end product, but rather it can be a model of your idea created quickly and easily to present your idea in a visual way that enables others to understand it and provide feedback on it.) Bringing your idea to life will help you think about it more deeply and find the gaps in your planning.

You want to prototype your idea and test it before investing a lot of money in implementing it because it is cheaper, easier, and quicker to make changes to a prototype. Making changes to existing infrastructure, product, or service already widely used by people can be very difficult and expensive.

Your prototype can be a drawing of your idea, a model, a short clip that demonstrates how your idea will work, or any other way that brings your idea to life and enables others to understand how it's going to work. The concept behind creating a prototype is to explain and communicate your idea to your target audience so you can get meaningful feedback on the proposed solution.

Testing your prototype will help you understand quickly whether your idea has the potential to work and what you need to change or add to your current idea. Then you can apply these changes to your prototype and test it again. By doing so, you create an iterative feedback loop that helps you design a product or service that provides value to your target audience quickly and cheaply.

You might find that your idea doesn't work, and you need to scrap it and move to your next idea. This is a good outcome, as in a short period of time and without investing much money, you've realised this is not a good solution, and you're able to move on to test another idea.

At times, it won't be easy to hear honest feedback on your prototype. Do your best not to take feedback as a personal criticism, as it has nothing to do with you as a person. That honest feedback, the kind you find difficult to digest, is probably the feedback you need to hear the most. This is probably the input that will help you most to improve and design a better product or service.

The more you seek this kind of honest feedback, the easier it gets to receive it. When I work with children, I find that at first, they perceive feedback as a personal attack. They think that if someone is providing them with suggestions for improvements, it means they did something wrong. But as they get used to working in this manner, as they understand the importance of such feedback, their perception of feedback transforms, and they start seeking it. They begin to appreciate feedback, as they know it helps them improve their ideas.

Ask your child to plan their prototype. Ask them to think about what they want to build and to draw their plan. This will set them up for a good start. It is also good to get them used to think and plan before they embark on a task.

Resist the temptation to let your child use complex and time-consuming ways to create prototypes (such as spending a few weeks creating a prototype on Minecraft). The idea behind this is to create a rough prototype and quickly get feedback on the idea. It is a way to show and explain your concept to others, so they can understand it and provide input. This is how you create an iterative loop for improvement to your idea.

In the same vein, when a child (or adult) spends a lot of time and effort on creating a prototype, they can develop an attachment to it. Due to this attachment, they are less open to receiving feedback and making changes to what they have created. So, spending a lot of time and effort on creating a prototype is counterproductive to what you want to achieve.

Before your child test their prototype with other people, have a conversation with them about feedback. Discuss the below questions:

- What is feedback?
- Why do we need feedback?
- What kind of feedback is useful and beneficial to us?

> "My students are more open to making improvements and adjustments. It [The creative process] is kind of giving them more high standards in their work; they don't settle anymore. They are building their standard up and are kind of happier to make improvements to a product."
> —Ashlee McCarthy, year 3 teacher at Edithvale primary school

Some Final Thoughts

It is important to understand that the creative process is not a linear one. Although the process has five defined stages—**R**esearch, **I**ncubate, **D**ream, **E**valuate, and **R**ealise (RIDER)—when you progress along this path, you might find you need to go back and revisit previous stages to progress further. Sometimes we need to take a few steps back to move forward. For example, when you **E**valuate ideas, you might find you need to do some more **R**esearch to progress with your evaluation. Or when you **R**ealise, you might find you need to go back to the **D**ream stage to brainstorm ideas based on your learning from testing your prototypes.

At times, you might find yourself overwhelmed. It might happen after **R**esearch when you need to make sense of piles of data. Or it might happen when you get stuck and can't come up with unique ideas during the **D**ream stage. When it happens, trust yourself and the process. Don't rush the process or yourself. Taking the time to Incubate will provide you with the needed break from working on your problem and will do you a lot of good. Step away and do something you enjoy doing, something that fills you with good energy. Come back to the problem once you are energised.

The Creative Process as a Learning Framework

The RIDER process is the perfect framework for any question or problem you want to explore with your child. Any question should start with **R**esearch, where you let your child drive the questions asked on the topic and the research itself. And then continue with the rest of the creative thinking process, as explained in this chapter. Use this framework to design and plan your child's learning.

To see more details about using the creative process as the framework for children's learning, I've provided an "in action" scenario in the next chapter. Seeing how this process is used within a home setting will help you understand how you can walk your child through the five stages of the creative thinking process, to help them learn and develop their innovative and creative mind.

Chapter Summary

- Creativity is a process, not a single event.
- This is the creative process: **RIDER** (**R**esearch, **I**ncubate, **D**ream, **E**valuate, and **R**ealise).
- Sharing knowledge, thoughts, and ideas are key to creativity.
- The creative process is nonlinear.

Reflective Questions

Reflect on the following questions to help you foster creative thinking in yourself and your child:

1. What might you change in your parenting style as a result of learning about RIDER?

   _____
   _____
   _____

2. How might you change your approach to problem-solving?

   _____
   _____
   _____

3. What might change in your approach to other people's perspectives, opinions, ideas, and beliefs?

   _____
   _____
   _____

CHAPTER 9:
THE CREATIVE PROCESS IN ACTION

> "Education is the most powerful weapon which you can use to change the world."
> - Nelson Mandela

This chapter focuses on
- The creative process in action

Learning new ways of thinking is one thing, but knowing how to implement this new learning in your life can be another thing altogether. Knowing the theory doesn't necessarily mean you know how to use it and what using it means for you. While in Chapter 8 you learnt the theory, you'll see that theoretical information "in action" in this chapter.

Whether you are homeschooling or your child attends a private or public school, I am sure you want to learn how to help your child develop an innovative mind. In this chapter, you will find an example of how you can use RIDER at home to help your child develop the essential skills for success.

What follows is a guide for using the creative thinking process as a framework for solving problems, exploring questions your child is curious about, working on family initiatives, or solving family challenges.

I've elaborated on how each of the five steps of the creative process can look within a home environment and how you can guide and work with your child through the different stages.

If you are looking for explicit instructions and a recipe for how to go about RIDER for each age group, I intentionally haven't provided them.

Think Unique takes you on your creative journey, develops your innovative thinking and empowers you to use RIDER in many ways. It empowers you to become a "chef" and create your own recipes.

As there are significant differences between children's capabilities, depending on their age and other factors, I leave it to you, the parent, to try out and decide what works best with your child. Feel free to dial it up or down as you see fit for your own family.

It is also up to you to decide if, how, and what kind of technology to incorporate. You can be creative and tailor the use of the RIDER process to your own circumstances and needs.

For parents interested in having a deeper dive into the creative thinking process in action, I got you covered. If you want to approach this process in a more structured way, for any educational setup, the elaborated example at the end of this book will be of value to you. So, when you are ready, read the section named - A Deep Dive into RIDER.

Applying the Creative Thinking Process

To start, there is a need to choose the question your child, you and your child, or the whole family will work on. It's important this question will be one that your child is curious about. (A curious mind is a mind that is ready to learn!) It needs to be relevant for them, impacts them, a question they care about, and something they feel invested in.

When children (and adults) feel connected to what they are working on, they are more engaged and make more of an effort. Engaged children learn better and also behave better.

Enabling your child to work on the right question for them empowers them to drive change and become caring, participating members of their communities.

So, what question should we use in this example?

Let's see the creative process in action while working on an important, real-world question related to something very close to our hearts- our family.

I believe the importance of spending time as a family won't come as a surprise to you.

We all know there are many benefits to spending time with our loved ones. Furthermore, this time together as a family is crucial for our children's development and wellbeing.

Children who grow up in families that spend time together:[1]

- are less stressed
- are more resilient
- are more confident
- have better mental health
- perform better academically
- have fewer behavioural issues
- are better at dealing with conflicts

The benefits of spending time as a family are not limited to our kids. Parents benefit greatly from spending time with their families too.

Spending time with your loved ones develops special bonds between family members and creates trust and beautiful memories.

With all these fantastic benefits you would think that we will make sure to spend a lot of time with each other. While this might be our desire, what we wish for our family and how we want to live our lives, the reality is sometimes quite different.

A study performed by Visit Anaheim on the time families spend together found that families spend only 37 minutes of quality time together per day[2]. Just 37 minutes!

There are a few significant reasons for this decline. Our lives are becoming more and more hectic, with parents:

- working more hours
- experiencing more stress
- handling packed kids' activities schedules

And with the non-stop presence of technology in our lives that creates constant interruptions, we spend less and less time as a family. If you raised your eyebrow now, wondering if your family enjoys more than 37 minutes of quality time together per day, there is something you need to be aware of. We often confuse the time we spend on screens while our family members are around as family time.

Research performed by Killian Mullan from Oxford University and Stella Chatzitheochari from the University of Warwick found that we spend more alone time together.[3]

As it turns out, families spend *more* time together than ever before. But it is not a together-together time. It is more of an alone-together time.

This alone-together time means that although our family members are at home together more than before, we spend this time doing activities on our own. Therefore, it is actually alone time and not family quality time.

You probably guessed correctly that a lot of this alone-together time is taken up by screens.

The good news is we can change it. If we want to strengthen our family relationships, cultivate our wellbeing, and have fun as a family, we can make it happen.

Therefore, let's say your child says they would like to do more things together, as a family.

As a result of this desire, the question we will explore in this chapter would be –

How might we spend more time as a family?

So, where do we start? As per our acronym RIDER, the starting point is the first stage of the creative process, **R**esearch.

Step 1: Research—The Starting Point

To perform thorough research, we need to start by exploring the question itself. In our example, *How might we spend more time as a family?* We need to start by understanding why it is an important question to explore.

When working on this question with your child, ask them why is it important to spend time as a family? Discuss it with your child.

Explore with your child the benefits of spending time together as a family. You can start this exploration as a discussion and then search this topic online. While exploring together, you can ask your child these questions-

- What type of activities do you like to do as a family? Why?
- What might prevent us from spending time together?
- Describe the best day with our family. What are we doing together that makes it so special?
- What makes you happy? Why?
- What makes you feel loved?

Once you and your child feel you have a good understanding of the importance of this question, ask your child if you need to involve other people in exploring *How might we spend more time as a family?*

When working on a problem, a topic, or any challenge, it is essential to involve everyone related to this problem or question in finding a solution.

In this case, it means involving all your family members.

(Since this topic is very much about your family's culture and way of engagement with each other, your child can lead the exploration of this question while all family members are involved throughout the RIDER process.)

Understanding different needs

A great way to understand the different family members' views on our question is by talking with them about it and asking them questions. (In a more formal setup, it is called interviewing) But before starting such conversations, your child will need to think about what questions they'll be asking.

To come up with questions to ask, your child will need to think about:

What do I want to understand and find out from my family about - *How might we spend more time as a family?*

This is a fantastic opportunity to discuss with your child the need to think about what they want to achieve from performing a particular activity, before they start it.

Approaching the research step in this manner will help your child understand the need to plan before taking action. (And planning always sets you up for a good start.)

For the question we explore, the things we want to understand from asking our family members questions might be:

1. What might prevent us from spending more time together,
2. What kind of activities we like to do as a family,
3. How might we spend more quality time as a family.

The Art of Asking Questions

Once your child is clear on what they want to understand from your family members, ask your child to suggest the questions they will need to ask to achieve this understanding.

But before your child can come up with different questions, it is time to chat about the type of questions that provide detailed answers. Successful research means getting the information required to understand the question or challenge at hand. This includes the needs, wants, challenges and desires of the people involved in this question. And to get all this information, your child will need to get detailed answers to their questions.

Therefore, let's explore the art of asking questions.

A question can be a closed-ended question, such as – Would you like to spend more time with your family?

Possible answers to these questions are – yes, no, maybe, I don't know.

As you can see, these are very short answers that don't provide much information.

Since this research aims to understand the different family members' needs, wants, and opinions, we need to ask questions that invite more detailed answers.

Consequently, your child will need to ask open-ended questions, such as this one-

What kind of activities would you like to do with our family?

This type of question invites an elaborated answer.

And when your child gets an answer to this question, they will need to follow up with whys, to gain a deeper understanding.

Let's look at an example.

Let's say your child asked their sibling the question – "What kind of activities would you like to do with our family?"

And the answer was – "I like to go on a bike ride and go to the beach".

As a result, your child learnt what kind of activities their sibling likes to do with your family, but they didn't find out *why* they like them.

Now let's look at how much more understanding you can get when you follow up with a why.

Your child (The one that drives the exploration of this question) - "What kind of activities would you like to do with our family?"

The sibling - "I like to go on a bike ride and go to the beach".

Your child – "Why do you like to go on a bike ride as a family?

The sibling – "Because I like it when we stop at different places and do fun things together. Sometimes we stop at a coffee shop, and I get to have a milkshake or a cake. Sometimes we stop at a playground, and we play together. Every time we go on a bike ride, we do different things and have fun. It is like going on an adventure."

As you can see, when you follow up an answer with a *why*, you gain a deeper understanding of the person you are having this conversation with. You learn more about their motivations, needs, behaviour, and their actions.

It is important to note that there is a balancing act between asking *why* to find out more and asking too many whys. When we ask too many whys, one after another, the other person might feel uncomfortable with it.

You can also ask why on another day or during another stage of the process if you feel you need to get more information.

Coming up with Questions

Let's return now to planning the questions to ask your family members. As mentioned earlier, this is what we want to understand by asking questions:

- What might prevent us from spending more time together,
- What kind of activities we like to do as a family,
- How might we spend more quality time as a family.

Now it's time for your child to develop a few questions that will help them gain this understanding.

These questions might be:

1. Once you finish work or school, what activities do you do until you go to sleep? How much time, roughly, do you spend on each activity?

2. What type of activities do you do during weekends? How much time, roughly, do you spend on each activity?
3. Thinking about the previously mentioned activities, what can you do differently to allow for more family quality time?
4. What type of activities do you wish to do with our family? Why?
5. Thinking about our family, what might come in the way of us spending more quality time together? Why?
6. As a family, what do we need to do differently to have more time together during weekdays?
7. As a family, what do we need to do differently to have more time together during weekends?

Now that your child has a set of questions, they will need to chat with each family member and ask them these questions. Ask your child to write down the answers each one provides.

Exploring the answers

Now that your child has answers from your family, it is time to explore these answers. Your child should search for similarities and differences in these answers to understand your family's activities, needs, challenges, and desires.

Let's look at a few examples of how to go about it:

Example #1 for the question - What type of activities do you wish to do with our family? Why?

Let's say a few answers are:

1. "I like to go on a bike ride because I like it when we stop at different places and do fun things together. Sometimes we stop at a coffee shop, and I get to have a milkshake or a cake. Sometimes we stop at a playground, and we play together. Every time we go on a bike ride, we do different things and have fun. It is like going on an adventure."

2. "I like going on nature walks as we get to talk a lot and laugh together."
3. "I like going bowling together because we get to compete with each other, joke when someone is missing a strike by one pin, and it is fun."
4. "I like cooking dinner together as I often choose what to make, and I get to try different things in the kitchen."
5. "I like making cookies together as it is fun making the dough, creating the shapes and then decorating the cookies together."

Your child will then need to look at and compare these answers to find patterns and points of difference.

In this example, we can see two patterns:

1. Our family loves doing physical activities together as we laugh and have fun together.
2. Our family loves cooking together as we enjoy experimenting together in the kitchen.

Example #2 for the question - Once you finish work or school, what activities do you do until you go to sleep? How much time, roughly, do you spend on each activity?

Let's say a few answers are:

1. "I prepare dinner for about one hour, I watch TV for about three hours, I eat dinner for about thirty minutes, I spend one hour on Facebook."
2. "I do homework for about one hour, I play Fortnite for about two hours, I eat dinner for about thirty minutes, I play Minecraft for about one hour, I play soccer for about one hour."
3. "I tidy the house for about one hour, I walk the dog for about forty minutes, I read for about one hour, I eat dinner for about thirty minutes, I spend one hour on social media, I watch TV for about two hours."

Your child will need to look at and compare these answers to find patterns and points of difference.

In this example, we can find these patterns:

1. We spend about one hour on weekdays doing chores.
2. We spend at least three hours on screens every day.
3. Every day we spend thirty minutes together when we are having dinner.

Ask your child to write down the patterns they have found in the answers to each of their questions.

Skills Being Developed

When performing the **R**esearch stage in this manner, your child develops the following skills:

- Understanding the differences between open-ended and closed-ended questions
- Able to think about what they want to get out of performing an activity
- Able to come up with questions that would help them learn and understand the topic they are exploring
- How to find patterns in different answers
- Empathy
- Curiosity
- Collaboration
- Verbal communication

Step 2: Incubate—Allow Time to Digest

At this stage in the creative process, your child has a chance to reflect on what they have learnt through the research they have performed and connect different pieces of information in their brains. Teachers and parents I've worked with have found that they need to give children time to ponder a question; they can't expect children to come up with answers right away. These parents are now aware that children will need time to digest a question, a period of incubation, and that some allowance for time to reflect needs to be part of the process.

As preparation for the incubation stage, ask your child to go over the answers they received to their questions and the patterns they have found in them.

The incubation time is the time your child needs to spark their thinking and creativity.

Researchers have found one simple way to do this, and that is for your child to take a break from thinking about the question they explore. People who take a break, or incubate, can come up with not only more ideas but also more unique ideas than people who don't take a break.[4]

Further, the type of activity you perform during your incubating time influences the effectiveness of this break on your creativity. There are three types of breaks you can take:

1. Break with no specific task to perform.
2. Break with an undemanding task for your brain.
3. Break with a demanding task for your brain.

As the research shows, people who performed an undemanding task during the incubation period outperformed those who did the demanding task or no task at all.[5] This is because when you take a break without performing any tasks, your conscious mind is still contemplating the original problem you want to solve. When you take a break by doing a demanding task for your brain, your brain needs to focus on performing that task. This, in turn, prevents your brain from switching into an "idle" state that will enable your subconscious mind to think about your original problem.

To summarise, for a time of incubation to have a positive impact on creative thinking, your conscious mind needs to work on an undemanding task during a break, while your subconscious mind works on creating new connections to solve the problem or question you are exploring.

Let's look now at the length of the incubation time. The incubating period depends on the complexity of the problem. The more complex the problem is, the more time required for incubation. In terms of incubating time for your child, let them spend some time doing other activities they enjoy and check in with them after a while to see whether they are ready to come up with ideas for solutions.

In terms of what type of activity to choose for this purpose, it is best to select a task very different from your original problem.[6] This undemanding task can be as simple as tidying up the house, building a tower from different materials, jumping on the trampoline, or going for a walk.

You can take time for incubation during the next stage, *Dream,* if you feel that your child has provided ideas and then got stuck. When they can't develop more ideas, a break with an undemanding task can help them generate new ideas.

Step 3: Dream—Brainstorm Ideas

This is the time to come up with ideas on how to solve the question you are exploring. Children love coming up with ideas to solve a problem, even more so when it's a real-world problem that impacts them.

For the question we explore in this chapter, it would be fantastic if all family members brainstormed ideas.

Go over the brainstorming rules with everyone as listed in Chapter 8 for Step 3, Dream, on page 118. (You can download these rules at www.glitteringminds.com.au/resources). As the parent, make sure everyone adheres to the rules to have a safe environment to express ideas.

It's important to remember that there are no right or wrong ideas when brainstorming ideas. Any idea is welcomed!

You can brainstorm ideas over dinner or at any other setup where your family members are relaxed and ready to spend some fun time together. Make sure to write down all the ideas everyone comes up with.

Encourage your family members to build on each other's ideas and to let their imaginations run wild. As an example, here are a few ideas for solutions to the question, "How might we spend more time as a family?":

1. A few times a week cook dinner together.
2. Ban the use of mobile phones during dinner.
3. Make sure everyone eats dinner together.
4. Once a week have a board game night.
5. Go on a bike ride during weekends.
6. A few times a week go to the park together.
7. Have a "no screens" night once a week.
8. Rest when you get home after work.
9. Split the house chores between more family members.
10. Use deliveries instead of going to the shops.

 If your family members get stuck, or you feel their ideas are trivial and there is a need to dig deeper for more innovative ideas, you may want to take them further by introducing "crazy ideas" and letting them build on these ideas. For example:

1. Getting rid of all our screens.
2. Go on a family holiday every weekend.
3. Stop working.

4. Stop going to school.

Let's see how your family members can take two of these crazy ideas and build on them.

Crazy idea #1: Go on a family holiday every weekend. The essence of this idea is that when we are on holiday, we don't spend time on chores and errands and have a lot of time as a family.

While it would be fantastic to go on a holiday every weekend, it is probably not a viable option financially. However, what we can do, is bring the holiday into our home. What I mean by that is that we can pretend we are on a holiday while staying at home. We can decide that we are not doing any chores and errands during this weekend. We can spend all of the time as a family, doing things together. We can even go camping in our living room, tell each other campfire stories while using a torchlight, and play cards.

Crazy idea #2: Stop working. The concept here is for parents to have more time with their family. For parents to free more space in their lives, to make their lives less busy and less tiring.

Here's how this concept can be applied: Check whether you can work less. There are different ways to reduce your working hours– reduce commute time, become more efficient, create clear boundaries between working time and home time, etc.

If you simply feel tired after a day at work, think about what can re-energise you before you come home to your family and do it.

If you need to clear your mind from work to be fully present with your family, explore ways to disconnect from work while you are with your loved ones.

We now have these additional ideas to add to our list:

1. Have a holiday at home.
2. Create clear boundaries between work and home time.

When performing the **D**ream stage in this manner, your child develops the following skills:

- Collaboration
- Empathy
- Creative thinking
- Creative confidence
- Verbal communication
- How to brainstorm ideas

Step 4: Evaluate

Once you complete the **D**ream stage, it's time to choose an idea to bring to life.

Your child can start this stage by grouping similar ideas, or you can do it as a family. This helps reduce the number of ideas you will need to choose from.

In this step, your family members will need to vote on their favourite ideas.

Decide as a family if you want to vote on the top idea, the top two ideas or maybe the top three ideas.

It is up to you to decide how you want to go about it and how many ideas you would like to **R**ealise.

Have a discussion as a family on the practical aspects you need to consider when choosing ideas.

For the question we are exploring in this chapter, things to consider might be:

1. Can we really make it happen?
2. Will you agree to this? (Need to check if all family members will do it)

3. Will the result of doing this be more quality time as a family?

 This discussion is an opportunity for your child to practise their communication skills, critical thinking, and verbal persuasion techniques.

Once you finish voting on your top ideas, you will end up with the most favourite idea or the most two-three favourite ideas.

When performing the **E**valuation stage in this manner, your child develops the following skills:

- Collaboration
- Resilience
- Critical thinking
- Verbal persuasion
- Creative thinking
- Confidence
- Verbal communication
- How to evaluate ideas

Step 5: Realise—Bring Ideas to Life

Now it's time to plan how to incorporate the top idea (or ideas) into your family life.

Your child can work on this plan, or you can create it as a family. They can create a plan for the next month regarding what your family activities would look like. (One option is to create a calendar of activities.)

When your child has finished creating this plan, ask them to present the plan to the whole family. Discuss this plan as a family and ask for your family members' feedback.

Once everyone agrees on the plan, it is time to make it happen.

Follow the new plan and revisit it after a month. This is an opportunity for the whole family to provide feedback on how the new plan is going.

When providing feedback on the new family activities plan, think about:

1. Is this a good solution for the question we explored? If it is not, it is time to move on to another idea.
2. Is there a need to make changes and improve this plan? What is working well? What is not working well? What can be improved?

If needed, make changes to your plan based on your family feedback.

Then, create your plan for the next month.

You can revisit the plan again after another month. This can be an iterative process that enables you to keep improving your activities and happiness as a family.

When performing the **R**ealise stage in this manner, your child develops the following skills:

- Collaboration
- Resilience
- Critical thinking
- Creative thinking
- Confidence
- Verbal communication
- Presentation
- How to seek feedback
- How to improve your product/idea based on feedback

Chapter Summary

- The creative process is your framework for doing projects with your child.
- You can add your own creative flair to each of the creative process steps.
- There are significant differences between children's capabilities, depending on their age and other factors. Therefore, dial up or down the RIDER process, as you see fit for your own family.
- Using the creative process develops your child' twenty-first-century skills.
- Following the creative process creates a culture of innovation at your home.

Reflective Questions

After seeing the creative process in action, at home, take time to reflect on the questions below:

1. How can I apply the creative process at home?

    _____
    _____
    _____

2. How can I apply the creative process in my parenting beyond questions my child is curious about?

    _____
    _____
    _____

3. How can I use the creative process to tackle different challenges we have at home? (for example, children's behaviour)?

    _____
    _____
    _____

PART FOUR

PRACTICAL TOOLS AND EXERCISES TO DEVELOP CREATIVE THINKING

I am very proud of you as you have come a long way on your creative journey. By now you have learnt:

- what creativity is,
- why it is so important to develop creative thinking,
- what mindset and approaches are required for success,
- how to create an environment that promotes creativity and innovation,
- what the creative thinking process is and how to use it as a framework to plan and design projects at home.

And you developed your capabilities to:

- Develop your child's life skills and prepare them for success in the real world,
- Develop your child's innovative mindsets and potentially create the next Elon Musk or Bill Gates,
- Provide your child with mindset, process, and tools they can use to solve any problem.

This chapter is about continuing the journey to develop the most important skill to have today: creative thinking. You can continue to develop your own superpower and set up your child for success by taking them further along this journey.

All the activities in Part Four are designed for both adults and children. You can do these activities on your own, with your family, your colleagues as fun activities during staff meetings, or in any other setting.

All the activities in Chapter 10 can be downloaded from here: https://www.glitteringminds.com.au/resources.

You might want to recall from Part Three that the following emojis are used to indicate the level of difficulty for each exercise in Part Four:

 Weight-lifting emojis mark an exercise. There are three levels of difficulty. When you see one emoji lifting weights, this is an entry-level exercise—anyone can do it.

 Two weight-lifting emojis indicate the exercise is a bit more advanced. Young children who are starting their creative-thinking journey might need to wait until they progress further along the journey to do these exercises. If you want to check whether your child can tackle this level, let them try it out and gauge how they cope with it.

 Three weight-lifting emojis indicate the exercise is much more advanced. These exercises are more appropriate for teenagers and adults due to the complexity of the thinking involved. However, for certain gifted younger children, these exercises will be a good way to stretch their thinking skills.

CHAPTER 10:

IMAGINATION

> "Imagination is more important than knowledge. For knowledge is limited, whereas imagination embraces the entire world, stimulating progress, giving birth to evolution."
> - Albert Einstein

This chapter focuses on
- The importance of imagination
- The impact of constraints on imagination and creativity
- How to develop your imaginative superpowers

The ability to imagine is a wonderful and very special gift. With the power of your imagination, you can travel back in time, to the future, to made-up places, and even into faraway galaxies.

All children love to imagine. When my children were very young, I used to buy them different toys. Some of these toys were appealing visually and had lots of colourful buttons to trigger different functions. Some were quite expensive to purchase, but like any other parent, I felt that investing money in toys that would help my children's development was a good investment to make. But even though my boys were surrounded by what I thought to be amazing toys, they still preferred to play with a cardboard box and turn it into whatever their imagination came up with.

I still remember how a delivery box filled with an abundance of compostable packing peanuts kept them busy for days on end. This box turned into a bus, a train, a space shuttle, a tent, and a bathtub to name just a few.

As a child, one of my favourite activities was to lie on the grass, look up at the clouds, and imagine different shapes moving across the sky. I would often see mythological creatures in the cloud formations, and I could have done it for hours. I still enjoy this activity today.

At some point, as we grow older, most of us are told not to "waste time" on imagining things or "doing nothing." We get the message that these kinds of activities are a waste of time, and we should be doing something better, more productive. So as adults, we rarely spend time letting our imagination run wild, daydreaming, and having fun with it. This is a shame, as imagination goes hand in hand with creativity.

It's not too late to reignite the power of your imagination. Let your imagination take the steering wheel and trust it will take you to amazing places.

So, let's start! Here are a few activities to get your and your child's imaginations going.

If you haven't done these kinds of activities for a while, it might feel strange at first. Keep going, don't let that feeling stop you.

Exercise 1: Develop your imagination— Scribble your imagination

A simple activity to develop imagination is to take a random scribble and draw something from it. You can turn this scribble into anything you want. You are limited only by your imagination. The drawing doesn't need to make sense; it doesn't need to be something that already exists in your world. There are no limitations. Simply let your imagination run wild without any judgment. Try not to think and evaluate what you are going to draw. Don't stop to think about whether it makes sense. Just flow with your imagination and draw your own awesome picture. (I know you can do it!)

You can also use letters from the alphabet as a scribble exercise. It can help young children get familiar with the alphabet in a fun way.

Here are some samples of what some children drew when given this exercise. It is wonderful to see how each child created something different from the same scribble they were given.

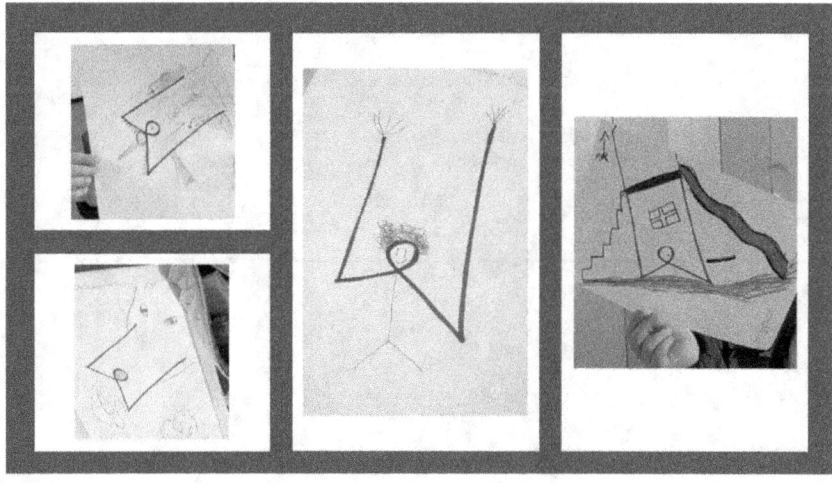

Exercise 2: Develop your imagination—Combine two shapes to tell a story from your imagination

This activity is similar to Exercise 1, but there are additional parameters to work with. Here you are asked to join two different shapes to create a new drawing and then tell a story from your imagination about the new drawing. In Exercise 1, you were given complete freedom to turn a scribble into whatever you wanted, but in this activity, you are given a constraint. You will need to use your imagination within boundaries.

Once you have turned the two shapes below into one picture, ask yourself: What is the story behind this drawing?

Here is an example of this exercise. The story in this drawing is of a night train ride, where passengers enjoy the starry sky.

Exercise 3: Develop your imagination—Shape your drawings

This activity is about using your imagination within even more boundaries.

Here are the instructions:

- You can use each shape as many times as you would like in your drawing.
- Use only the provided shapes to create the new drawing. (Don't add anything else.)
- Each shape should be used at least one time in your drawing.
- You can make the shapes larger or smaller.

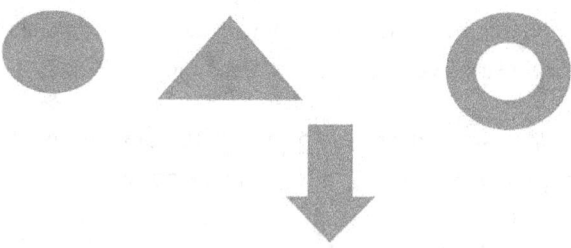

Here is an example of this exercise:

As you probably noticed, I've added boundaries and constraints as we progressed with different exercises to develop your imagination. There is a good reason to add boundaries and constraints when you want to flex your imagination and creative muscles.

To explore this concept, I want you to think of ideas for a new game. You have no limitations on what this might be. Stop reading and take a couple of minutes now to come up with some new game ideas.

How did you find the experience of coming up with new game ideas, given as an assignment without any boundaries? How many new games did you come up with?

Given a free hand, no boundaries at all, and being instructed to imagine whatever you wanted to without limitations was probably challenging. This is because such open-ended freedom can get in the way of the process of coming up with new ideas.

Most people struggle to come up with ideas when there is no framing for those ideas. It's too big a space to work with and can be overwhelming. Having too much freedom can cause you to struggle to do it at all, paralysing your ability to imagine new things.

Let's see what happens when we change the instructions to imagine a new game using only these items: a bucket, a rope, and a beach ball. Stop reading and take a couple of minutes now to come up with new game ideas using these items.

How did you find the experience of coming up with new game ideas while having some boundaries? How many ideas did you come up with? Was it easier for you to imagine a new game within the boundaries given to you?

I'm quite sure you came up with at least two ideas for a new game using these items.

As it happens, it's easier to imagine, to come up with new ideas, when you have clear boundaries to work with. Having boundaries helps you focus your thoughts and creativity within a given framework.

Having clear boundaries means you have a clear definition of the problem you wish to solve. When the problem is clear, it's much easier to come up with different, creative solutions.

Dr Caneel Joyce researched the effect of having constraints on creativity[1]. In this study, Dr Joyce explored the effect of choice—how not giving a choice and giving too much choice both impact creativity. She found a sweet spot that increases creativity, where just enough constraint drives us to come up with new ideas and possibilities.

It might feel counter-intuitive to you, but having constraints and obstacles increases your creativity. Creativity loves constraints. We should welcome constraints and look at them as an opportunity to come up with innovative ideas.

Framing a Problem with Its Constraint

Sweden has one of the highest numbers of cyclists globally and a high number of bicycle-related injuries and deaths per year. Apparently, knowing the risk of injury or death doesn't serve as a good incentive for Swedish cyclists to wear a helmet while cycling. When researching why this was the case, researchers found that people thought traditional helmets were ugly and uncomfortable. They also didn't want to step into work or a social event with "helmet hair."

The notion of wearing a helmet was negative, and one cyclist articulated it well by saying, "I think it would have to be invisible for me to want to wear it."

When Sweden passed a new law in 2005 mandating all children under fifteen wear a helmet when cycling, adults thought they would be mandated next to do the same. So, it was time to do something about the perception and resistance to wearing a helmet. This is when industrial design graduate students Terese Alstin and Anna Haupt decided to team up and investigate this problem.

Alstin and Haupt looked at the problem: Many cyclists are refusing to wear helmets due to the current design and the helmet's effect on the hairstyle. They framed the problem with its constraint: How might we design a helmet not worn on your head?

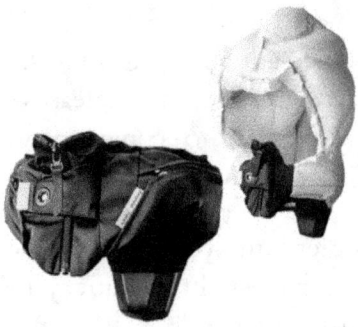

Defining this problem with its constraint provided an opportunity to come up with creative ideas. The result of this creative thinking was the development of an innovative product.

The team designed a prototype of an "invisible helmet," a helmet to be worn around the neck. This helmet has "smart" programmed sensors. When it senses that the cyclist's body movement is abnormal (as when they are about to have an accident), it deploys an inflatable nylon hood around the cyclist's head. This is similar to how airbags in a car are inflated to protect you from an impact.

Chapter Summary

- Imagination is a gift you should treasure and develop.
- Having boundaries and a clearly defined problem helps creative thinking.
- Constraints are opportunities to be imaginative and creative.

Reflective Questions

Now that you are aware of the importance of developing and using your imagination, it's time to incorporate using your imagination into your daily life.

Take time to reflect on the following questions:

1. How might you incorporate imaginative thinking into your current everyday tasks?

   _____
   _____
   _____

2. What might you change in your parenting approach to help your child develop their imagination?

   _____
   _____
   _____

3. How might you dedicate some time during your day or week for daydreaming?

   _____
   _____
   _____

CHAPTER 11:

WHAT IF...?

> "It is what we know already that often prevents us from learning."
> - Claude Bernard, French physiologist

This chapter focuses on
- The surprising effect of having knowledge
- The need to break free from our knowledge
- The ways to overcome limiting thinking

Now that you know you are creative, let's look at one important barrier to creative thinking and how we can overcome it.

We all value knowledge and rightly so. Having knowledge is powerful in many ways. It enables us to understand the world around us, grow professionally and personally, and positively impact our environment.

Acquiring knowledge is crucial to our survival. Therefore, from the moment you are born, you are busy learning and exploring the things around you and how these things work. You do so to create your own mental model of the world.

A mental model is a framework you create in your mind to reduce complexity and make sense of things. You use your created framework in everything that you do. This is how you look at the world around you and approach solving problems. And we can have more than one mental model. Having these mental models helps you survive and thrive in the world.

I believe that most people will agree with me on the importance of acquiring knowledge. Having said that, when it comes to creativity, knowledge can be a double-edged sword. This is because once you know the purpose of different things around you, it can become difficult to let go of this knowledge and look at the world with fresh eyes.

Armed with knowledge, we are often fixed on "what is" and how things "should be," and by doing so, we close our minds to different perspectives, new ideas, and new possibilities.

It might surprise you to realise that being an expert can limit your ability to come up with unconventional solutions to problems in your field of expertise. It may sound counter-intuitive that an expert in a field is limited in their thinking, so I will explain why and how it happens.

When you become an expert, your knowledge in that field is deep and wide. You have been learning and working in it for many years, and your mind is set on specific ways of thinking and approaching problems. You are "programmed" to think in a specific way. You have rules that you follow. You have specific expectations for how things should be working, and this mindset narrows your thinking. It becomes difficult to see beyond your expertise and experience.

The phenomenon of having a set way of thinking that acts as a barrier for coming up with creative ideas to solve a problem is a known one. It is referred to as the "Einstellung effect." (*Einstellung* means "setting" or a person's "attitude" in German.)

Companies understand today that their ability to innovate is the core driver of growth and performance. Therefore, companies are investing billions in their internal ability to innovate, such as creating innovation incubators and accelerators.

With all this money spent on innovation, you would think these companies would be pleased with their levels of innovation. It turns out that even with a huge amount spent on innovation, 65 per cent of executives are dissatisfied with their company's ability to innovate[1].

Why is this happening? How do companies spend so much money on innovation and still not achieve their goals? A big part of the answer is that a specific group of employees works on innovation- related initiatives, and these employees share similar ways of thinking. It is the Einstellung effect in action, which inhibits innovation.

As a way to break free from this barrier, the concept of crowdsourcing ideas and solutions has been developed. This is the concept of seeking ideas and solutions for problems (at times, very complex problems) from a large group of people. The group can be all of the employees in a company, all of the customers, or anyone who is interested in providing their ideas and solutions. Crowdsourcing ideas is achieved by publishing the problem or challenge online.

Great ideas can come from anywhere and anyone. Crowdsourcing ideas enables anyone to bring their unique thinking forward. The approach of sharing challenges with a crowd enables companies to tap into diverse perspectives and unexpected ideas. It can also mean finding an innovative solution faster.

Today, there are crowdsourcing platforms where organisations can publish their challenges and often offer a monetary reward for the person or group of people who solve their challenges. One example of such a crowdsourcing platform is InnoCentive.

For companies, publishing their challenges on a crowdsourcing platform means innovating faster with lower cost and less risk. Big names such as Astra Zeneca, NASA, and Novartis find solutions to their complex problems on such platforms by crowdsourcing the challenges they struggle to solve.

A great example of the power of diverse thinking and the barrier to creative thinking resulting from experts' thinking can be seen in the challenge that Harvard's Clinical and Translational Science Centre published on the InnoCentive platform.

The Harvard Centre was trying to create an effective treatment for type 1 diabetes. You can imagine that many great, world-renowned experts were working on this project. Some of these Harvard researchers wanted to understand what areas they needed to research about type 1 diabetes. They thought that to develop an effective treatment for type 1 diabetes, they needed to learn more about the condition itself. They wanted to start with the question: "What do we not know to cure Type I diabetes?"

But the rest of Harvard researchers working on this project advised against it as they said they already had the knowledge required to produce an effective treatment.

Despite the difference of opinions between these two groups of Harvard researchers, the challenge of discovering what they don't know by asking the question: "What do we not know to cure Type I diabetes?" ran anyway on InnoCentive platform.

Publishing this challenge proved to be a huge success. Despite many Harvard researchers believing publishing this challenge on InnoCentive would produce no results, there were 195 submissions, and 12 winners have been identified[2].

As a result of this challenge, Harvard researchers gained new knowledge and understanding on this condition from people who had diabetes and their caregivers. This new knowledge led them to new directions to create an effective treatment for type 1 diabetes.

Crowdsourcing ideas is a powerful way to unlock innovation, but before you rush to publish your challenge on such a platform, you can take steps to bring on the desired beginner's mindset. There is a way to break free from the boundaries imposed by knowledge, and step into an open and creative mind. In the next four chapters, I'm going to show you how to do it.

To break free from barriers to thinking, you need to think differently, think unique. You need to leave behind the kinds of thoughts that anchor you in *what is*—thoughts like, *This is how it is done, This is how it should be, This is how it works, This is impossible*, and *This will never work*.

To be creative, you need to open your mind and embrace the different, the new, the opposite, and the impossible. You need to be asking, *What if…?*

The Four What if…? Questions

In the following chapters, I'll take you through exercises and activities to help you and your child practise asking these four *What if…?* questions and find solutions to problems using creative thinking. (These four *What If…?* questions are part of the downloadable resources of this book. You can find them at www.glitteringminds.com.au/resources.)

1. **Repurposing:** What if we use this product, service, process, or concept for a different purpose in a different way?
2. **Merging:** What if we merge these products, services, processes, or concepts?
3. **Improving:** What if we improve this product, service, process, or concept?
4. **New Ways:** What if we take a concept and find a new way to go about it? Or what if we come up with a new concept?

Chapter Summary

- When it comes to creative thinking, having knowledge can be a double-edged sword.
- The Einstellung effect is a phenomenon in which experts have a set way of thinking, and therefore cannot come up with different ideas and approaches to solve problems.
- Crowdsourcing ideas and solutions is a way to tap into diverse thinking and find innovative solutions to problems.
- By opening your mind and asking, "What if...?" you can overcome the Einstellung effect and develop your creative thinking.

Reflective Questions

You are now aware of the role your knowledge and experience play in your ability to come up with creative ideas and look at a problem from different perspectives. As the saying goes, understanding the problem is half of the solution.

To bring this awareness into your life, reflect on the following questions:

1. Do you sometimes automatically come up with responses to problems without thinking deeply, exploring the facts, and examining different perspectives and angles?

   _____
   _____
   _____

2. When you need to think about solutions for a problem, do you prefer experts' ideas and opinions vs people who have less experience or no experience in the field of this problem?

   _____
   _____
   _____

3. How might you approach problem-solving in an opposite way to how you usually think?

   _____
   _____

CHAPTER 12:

WHAT IF...? — REPURPOSING

> "To repurpose an old thought, idea, or memory to a new purpose is the height of creativity."
> - Steve Supple, American designer

This chapter focuses on
- What Repurposing means
- The two ways to go about Repurposing
- How to develop your Repurposing superpowers

Repurposing is the ability to take an already existing product, service, concept, etc., and use it for a different purpose. It's about looking at what already exists and asking the question, What if I use this in a different way for a different purpose? It's about breaking free from thinking, *This is used for...* or *This is used in this manner...*.

Let's take the drone, for example. In 1916, a radio-controlled, pilotless aeroplane was created as a flying bomb to be piloted remotely at enemy targets. Over the years, the drone continued to be developed as a weapon. During the 1960s, radio-controlled drones became available for purchase by the public for recreational use. This opened the door to creative thinking about how a remote-controlled aircraft could be used for different purposes, including commercial ones.

Since then, people have come up with many ideas on how drones can be used for different purposes. Here are a few ways drones are used today:

- planting trees,
- wildlife conservation,
- finding people during rescue missions,
- providing medical supplies for people in disaster areas,
- window cleaning,
- light shows,
- predicting the weather,
- providing first aid,
- pesticide crops

Two Ways to Repurpose

You can arrive at Repurposing from two different angles:

1. I think that this product, service, process, or concept can be used in a different way, for a different purpose.
2. I have a problem I need to solve. What existing products, services, processes, or concepts can I use to solve this problem?

An example of the first type of Repurposing is the story of Playdough. Playdough was originally created as a wallpaper cleaner, and it worked great for that purpose. It didn't contain any toxins, was reusable, and did a great job at cleaning stains from wallpapers. Teachers in classrooms found a different use for the wallpaper cleaner. They found it could work very well as a modelling compound and for arts and crafts projects. Children could easily shape the soft wallpaper cleaner with their hands and turn it into whatever shape they desired.

Due to teachers' creative thinking, a wallpaper cleaner was repurposed as a modelling tool for children. It was given a new name, Playdoh, and marketed to schools and toy shops.

An example of the second type of repurposing is the story of how the organisation Design That Matters used car parts to build a baby incubator. Around the world, about 2.5 million babies die every year, shortly after birth[1]. Using a baby incubator could save many of them. In developing countries, the infant mortality rate is higher than in developed countries. This is due to the high cost of purchasing and maintaining the high-tech incubators that keep babies alive. Developing countries often don't have the funds for such lifesaving equipment.

A team of designers wanted to find a way to do the following: 1) build a baby incubator cheaply, and 2) build a baby incubator that local people would be able to maintain without additional training. They investigated the materials available in these countries that could be used to build an incubator. They discovered cars are a common product and that many local people knew how to fix cars. So, they repurposed the use of car parts and built a baby incubator from those. By doing so, they ensured the ability of local people to maintain the incubators, and therefore, safeguarded the ongoing use of baby incubators made this way to save lives.

 Here are a few questions to think about when Repurposing:

1. What else can an existing product, service, process, or concept be used for?
2. What existing product, service, process, or concept can I Repurpose to solve my problem?
3. How would a child use that existing product? How would an older person use it?

4. How would people with different disabilities use it?
5. How would an alien from outer space use it?
6. What would be some silly ways to use it?
7. What would be some crazy ways to use it?

Repurposing Products

It is easy to practise this type of creative thinking by Repurposing products you use in your everyday life. You can do these exercises with your family members. It will help them develop their creative thinking and innovative mindset. Here are a few examples of regularly used products and some activities to guide you in repurposing them.

Exercise 4: Repurposing—A spaghetti server

Look at a spaghetti server and try to come up with as many ideas as you possibly can for different uses of this item. If you are doing it with your family, start off doing it as an individual task, each person coming up with as many ideas as they possibly can on their own. Each can write or draw their ideas and then share them with others. When you finish sharing, it's time to see if anyone has more ideas. Try to develop more ideas by building on each other's ideas.

You can do this exercise with any object, such as an umbrella, a cup, or a shoe. You can ask your child to choose a random object, and then all family members will need to come up with ideas on how this object can be repurposed.

Exercise 5: Repurposing—Reuse or upcycle used items

Reusing objects helps us develop our creativity while looking after our environment. It is great to get children to think about how to reuse objects instead of throwing them away.

Follow the guidance for the activity in Exercise 4 to come up with ideas on how to repurpose and reuse—old bikes, old tennis rackets, old barrels, used tyres, old piano, and any other used product.

You can also use this exercise with your family members to find creative ways to decorate your home using used items.

Exercise 6: Repurposing—Cat stuck in a tree

Your cat is stuck in a tree. You can't reach your cat by stretching your arms or climbing up on the tree without aids. You don't have a ladder, and now you need to improvise a way to rescue your cat.

How can you rescue your cat by using things you have at home?

Exercise 7: Repurposing—Dragon costume

You are invited to a costume party and need to dress up as a dragon. The party is tomorrow. You don't have a dragon costume at home, and you don't have time to buy one.

How can you create a dragon costume using what you have at home?

You can create similar stories as exercises for your child to help them develop the skill most desired by employers. There are endless opportunities to practise Repurposing products, whether you are at home, or out and about.

Repurposing Services

Repurposing can be applied to different services. A service used in one area can be Repurposed in a different area to provide new value. Following is an example of Repurposing the service of borrowing books from a library to another use.

Parents today value having different kinds of toys for their children. They see toys as a way to help their children learn and entertain themselves. As a parent, you know that children's fascination and interest in a new toy fades away quite quickly, and purchasing toys can be costly, both financially and for the environment.

Due to the above, the library service of making a book available to borrow, read, return, and then get another book (instead of having to purchase these books), has been repurposed for toys. There are now toy libraries where parents can borrow toys for a few weeks and then return them and borrow a different toy.

Exercise 8: Repurposing—Party bus service

Use your creative thinking to repurpose the party bus service. How might you repurpose this service model for another use? A couple of ideas to get you started are a portable coffee shop and a mobile recording studio. See how many ideas you and your family members will come up with.

Repurposing Concepts and Ideas

Repurposing can be applied to concepts and ideas. The cross-pollination of concepts from one area of life to a completely different area can drive amazing innovation and value.

Following is an example of Repurposing a concept from race cars to hospital care.

What is the connection between a race car pit stop and a hospital's intensive care unit? At first glance, it seems these two activities are not even remotely connected. How can a race car pit stop be anything like an intensive care unit where doctors and nurses save lives?

Practical Tools and Exercises to Develop Creative Thinking | 179

But when you look closely, you see similarities between the process of handing over a patient from a theatre room to an intensive care unit and what happens at the pit lane. Just like at a pit stop, such a hospital transfer requires a highly coordinated, efficient, and fast-working team.

If you've ever seen a pit stop crew in action, you may have noticed how well the team is organised. Every team member knows exactly what they need to do, and they don't waste a millisecond. They act as a team to do what needs to be done as quickly as possible. Watching a pit stop crew at work feels like watching a performance of an Olympic gold medal synchronised swim team.

A few years back, when doctors looked at videos from pit stop activity and compared what they saw to a video of a patient transfer in the hospital, they were shocked to see how much the hospital handover tended to be chaotic and disorganised. There was a clear contrast between the efficient work of the pit stop crew and the way the hospital crew worked. It became clear the skills developed for race car pit stops could help save lives at hospitals.

As a result, hospitals learnt from pit stop crews how to go about patient transfers and changed the way their teams' work. They learnt how to predict what might go wrong and be prepared for it[2].

Another example of repurposing a concept is how the McDonald brothers improved their restaurant. They repurposed the assembly line idea used by Ford Motors to mass-produce cars to prepare hamburgers, and by doing so, transformed the fast-food industry.

Exercise 9: Repurposing— Make your own product

You might be familiar with Build-A-Bear shops. If you are not, these are stores where you can design and build your own stuffed animal. There are a variety of different stuffed animals and accessories to choose from. Use your creative thinking to repurpose the concept of building your own product. Where else might this concept be beneficial and provide value?

Chapter Summary

- Repurposing is about looking at a product, service, process, concept, etc., and imagining, *What if I use it for a different purpose or in a different way?*
- You can arrive at Repurposing from two angles: using an existing thing differently or solving a problem using available existing items.
- You can practise Repurposing on everyday products.
- Allow yourself to get silly and crazy in your imagination as you come up with Repurposing ideas.

Reflective Questions

Now that you are aware of Repurposing as a way to develop your imagination, creative thinking, and innovative problem-solving, it's time to incorporate Repurposing into your daily life.

Take this opportunity to reflect on the following questions:

1. How might you incorporate Repurposing as part of your problem-solving process?

   _____

   _____

   _____

2. How might you help your child develop Repurposing as a way of thinking?

   _____

   _____

   _____

3. How might you develop your Repurposing thinking as an innovative way of thinking?

   _____

   _____

   _____

CHAPTER 13:
WHAT IF...? — MERGING

> "It's not what you look at that matters, it's what you see."
> - Henry David Thoreau, American naturalist, poet, and philosopher

> This chapter focuses on
> - What Merging means
> - How to develop your Merging superpowers

Merging refers to the ability to take two or more existing products or concepts and combining them to make something new. It means breaking free from thinking, *These things are not related to each other,* and instead finding new connections.

An example of Merging is in something we all use every day: the mobile phone and camera. These used to be two separate products until someone decided to combine them into one. Now we can't imagine having a mobile phone without the ability to take photos and videos as well!

Another example for Merging multiple products and concepts is the "Internet of Things" (IoT). IoT refers to merging the Internet with everyday devices—basically, any device that can be turned on and off. This is done by taking products like a kitchen oven, an air conditioner, a light bulb, or even a door, and adding sensors and Wi-Fi capabilities to these products. Then, by using an application that controls these sensors, you can turn these devices on and off from anywhere in the world.

And there you have it—now you can turn the lights in your child's bedroom on or off while you are not even at home. (Is it possible the IoT was originally invented as a way to play tricks on the people you love from afar?) You can turn on your air conditioner when you are still hours away, so you return home to a comfortable temperature. You can also unlock the front door to your house while out of town if you need to let a neighbour in to attend to an emergency without giving them a key in advance.

Merging, as a creative thinking exercise, can be practised at home, or wherever you are. You can Merge as many different things as you want.

 Here are a few questions to think about when using the Merging approach:

1. What ideas, features, processes, or people can I Merge?
2. What different materials or products can I Merge?
3. What can I Merge to create better value or a solution?
4. How can I Merge things that don't seem related to each other?

Here are a few exercises for you and your child to flex those creative muscles through Merging:

 **Exercise 10: Merging—Items**

Develop your creative thinking by merging two or more unrelated items. What if you merge a shoe and music into something new?

You can do this on your own or with your family. You can let each one generate their own ideas first and then share and create more ideas together, or you can brainstorm ideas together from the start.

Here are a few ideas that other people came up with for how to Merge a shoe and music:

- A shoe that plays sounds with each step.
- A shoe that plays music based on the pace of your walking or running.
- A shoe that plays music based on your mood.
- A shoe that plays music when you are hiking and changes the beat based on the terrain.

You can turn it into a fun game by asking your child to come up with two or more random items and then come up with ideas on how to Merge them.

Exercise 11: Merging—Random words

Practise your creative thinking by merging random words into a one-sentence story.

Generate five random words. (There are websites you can use for this purpose.) Then come up with a one-sentence story, using these five words.

Here is an example:

The five random words are Equal, Conservation, Kit, President, Float.

A one-sentence story is "As the president began to float back to sleep, she came up with the idea of a conservation kit that provides trees with equal rights to humans."

Be playful when you merge these words into a story.

Exercise 12: Merging—Songs

What if you merge two songs into one? Choose two songs you like and use your creative thinking to merge them into one great song. Sing the new song you have created!

Exercise 13: Merging—Stories

What if you merge different stories? Pick two of your favourite books or short stories and turn them into one fantastic story. Remember to be silly and have fun while you do this activity. You can give this exercise to your child as a fun activity to develop their literacy skills.

Exercise 14: Merging—Games

What if you merge two or more games? Choose any game to merge (board games, card games, sports games, or computer games). Develop your creative thinking by merging a few games and creating your new special game!

Your child will enjoy the opportunity to develop their creative thinking while creating new games. You can add to the fun by playing these new games they made.

Merging Services

It often makes good sense to merge a few services, as the audience that requires a specific service can benefit from having another service available at the same place and time.

A good example of this is merging a children's play centre with a coffee shop, creating a Play Café. Parents of young children want to take their children to safe areas where they can play. While the children are playing, it's ideal if parents also have a bit of peaceful time for themselves. (They deserve a bit of a break!) So, merging a children's play centre with a coffee shop makes a lot of sense and provides a lot of value to the customers.

Another example is cinemas. Many people who go to see a movie at a cinema purchase movie tickets as well as popcorn and drinks. Some cinemas require people to queue in one line to purchase movie tickets and then in another to buy sweets, popcorn, and drinks. But some cinemas have merged these two services, and now customers can purchase all from one place, meaning they only need to wait in one queue.

Exercise 15: Merging—Services at a supermarket

Use your creative thinking to think about which services you could merge to create a better experience for people at a supermarket. What other services can a supermarket offer its customers (on top of shopping for food and household items)?

Let your imagination run wild when you work on these exercises. There is no right or wrong idea. So, don't judge the ideas. Just let them flow and build on them. Be creative with your thinking and try to come up with some crazy ideas.

Exercise 16: Merging—Services at a restaurant

Use your creative thinking to think about which services you could merge to create a better experience for people when they dine at a restaurant. What other services can a restaurant offer its customers on top of serving food and drinks? What other services might a family need at a restaurant?

Merging Concepts and Ideas

Merging can also be for concepts and ideas. Merging different ideas and concepts is a powerful tool for innovation. Many new ideas are the result of combining a few ideas. In fact, unique ideas are often the result of merging ideas that seem unrelated to each other.

For example, Johannes Guttenberg combined the concept of the pressure created by a wine press with the concept of imprinting value on coins to create the printing press. Guttenberg merged these two seemingly separate ideas, and by doing so, started the printing revolution, and changed the whole world. (Think about mass production of printed books and the ability to spread knowledge quickly around the world. The invention of the printing press can be seen as the first internet!)

On a smaller scale, we can see the Merging of unrelated ideas in many diverse products. For example:

- Merging a children's scooter with a school bag.
- Merging a suitcase, a trolley, and something to sit and ride on as a ride-on suitcase for kids.
- Merging a watch with a pedometer, a heart rate monitor, and an exercise tracker to create the smartwatch.

You can practise and develop your creative thinking by picking a few ideas that seem unrelated to each other and come up with different ways to merge them to make something new.

Exercise 17: Merging—Two concepts

Use your creative thinking to merge the following concepts:

1. The concept of shared economy
2. The concept of sustainable living

Chapter Summary

- Merging means imagining how existing products, services, processes, or concepts can be merged to deliver better value or create something new.
- Merging means breaking free from thinking "these things are not related to each other."
- You can practise Merging with everyday objects.

Reflective Questions

Now that you are aware of Merging as a way to exercise your imagination and develop creative thinking and an innovative mindset, it's time to incorporate Merging into your daily life.

Take this opportunity to reflect on the following questions:

1. How might you incorporate Merging as part of your problem- solving process?

   _____
   _____
   _____

2. How might you help your child develop Merging as a way of thinking?

   _____
   _____
   _____

3. How might you develop your own thinking using Merging as an innovative way of thinking?

   _____
   _____
   _____

CHAPTER 14:

WHAT IF...? — IMPROVING

> "The biggest room in the world is the room for improvement."
> - Helmut Schmidt, German politician

> This chapter focuses on
> - Why Improving is so needed
> - What Improving is
> - How to go about Improving

There is no such thing as perfect—but there is always room for improvement. Whether it's a product, service, process, or concept, there is always a way to make it better.

In the world we live in, constant improvement is a must. The saying "if it ain't broke, don't fix it" is no longer applicable. The new phrase we need to adopt is "if you don't constantly improve, you'll be left behind."

The world is continuously moving forward, and so all aspects of life must move forward with it. Once products or services stop moving forward, they are actually moving backwards since the rest of the world is moving so quickly ahead. When products, services, or processes stand still and don't change, they become dated, and at some point, can become irrelevant.

It's amazing to realise that 88 per cent of the Fortune 500 firms that existed in 1955 are not on this list anymore[1]. Some went bankrupt, some merged with another, and some still exist but lost their position at the top because they stood still with their products and services. They didn't move forward with the times and failed to apply a continuous loop of improvements for their products and services, so they became irrelevant.

One example of this failure is the rental chain Blockbuster. Blockbuster used to be a movie and game rental giant. When the world moved to DVD rental delivery, Blockbuster failed to improve its services and offer delivery as well. Later, when the world moved from DVD delivery to online streaming, they still refused to Improve their services and kept holding on to their brick-and-mortar DVD rental stores. As a result of their refusal to constantly Improve and move forward with the rest of the world, they went under.

To make sure a product, service, or process continues to provide value and stays relevant, it needs to go through a continuous loop of Improvements.

Improving requires the ability to see the different parts of a product and identify the elements that create the whole. It is about breaking free from thinking, *This is how it has always been done, This is how it is built,* and *This is what people are used to.*

Once you can see and identify the different parts, whether it's a product, service, or process, you can rebuild that product differently. You can remove parts, add parts, make changes to parts, rearrange the parts, and create something that provides more value.

Improving a Process

Let's see how Improving is used to transform the shopping experience in recent years.

We all go to the supermarket to shop for food. It's clear to see that supermarkets have changed a lot in recent years. There used to be only one process for grocery shopping in the store:

1. Enter the supermarket and grab a trolley, if you need one.
2. Walk along the aisles and pick out whatever you need or want.
3. Go to a register where a cashier will scan your items, pack your groceries, and take your payment.
4. Grab your bags and leave the supermarket.

A few issues started to emerge with this process:

1. Customers had to wait in a queue to be served by a cashier.
2. Customers were not happy about the need to wait in a queue.
3. Some customers preferred to go about their shopping without having to interact with a cashier.

It soon became time to make improvements to this process, to look at different parts of the process and identify what needed to be changed. Now, as the result of an Improvement iteration, there is another way to go about grocery shopping:

1. Enter the supermarket and grab a trolley, if you need one.
2. Walk along the aisles and pick out whatever you need or want.
3. Go to a self-checkout stand where you will scan all your items, pack your groceries, and pay.
4. Grab your bags and leave the supermarket.

By Improving this process, customers have less wait time in queues and are therefore happier, the shopping process is more efficient, and the supermarket employees have more time to handle other tasks at the supermarket. This kind of improvement has spread to other areas in our daily lives, like the check-in process at airports, buying food at McDonald's, etc.

We see a further improvement of this process at Amazon Go stores. These are checkout-free stores. In these stores, Amazon uses technology that automatically detects when products are taken from or returned to the shelves and keeps track of them in a virtual cart. This enables customers to simply walk in, pick out what they want, and walk out. Later, Amazon sends the customer a receipt and charges their Amazon account. Amazon improved the grocery shopping process by removing the element of checking out completely from the process.

Improving a Product

Let's look now at how the approach of Improving is used to innovate when making a product. A car is a product most of us depend on and love to use. A car has many different parts and components to help it do what it needs to do, which is to take us from one place to another.

One of the critical components of a car is energy, and like our bodies, a car can't function without fuel for energy. For many years, gasoline was used as the only energy source for cars. During the 1970s, oil prices soared, and there was a shortage of gasoline. Due to these issues, people explored how to make improvements to the energy component of cars, and as a result, cars that used different sources of energy from gas were developed. Today some cars use alternative energy sources, such as electricity, hydrogen, natural gas, biodiesel, and Ethanol.

We often become so fixed on the way existing objects are assembled or how existing services are designed that we can't see past what already is. Therefore, we miss many new possibilities. But if we understand the different elements of something and how it works, we can improve specific components of it, and by doing so, we create more value.

 Here are a few questions to think about when taking the approach of Improving for a specific product:

1. What would happen if I removed a part?
2. What would happen if I rearranged the parts?
3. What can I substitute to make an Improvement?
4. What can I make bigger or smaller?
5. Can I add extra features?
6. How can I simplify it?
7. What is non-essential or unnecessary?
8. How can I substitute the time, people, place, or materials?
9. Can I change the colour, texture, sound, or shape?

Here are some exercises for you and your child to flex those creative muscles through Improving:

Exercise 18: Improving—A car

Let's look at the car below. What are the elements of this car? What are the different parts? Different parts include wheels, doors, a hood, windscreens, windows, mirrors, engine, headlights, bumper, etc.

What if we:

- rearrange parts of the car differently? (We might decide to move the headlights to different locations, maybe place them on top of the hood.)
- break down the engine into four smaller engines and place each one next to each wheel?

- move the location of the spare tyre?
- change the size of the rear-view mirrors and move them closer to the windows?
- move the engine to the back of the car?
- remove two out of the four headlights?
- remove the roof of the car?

Come up with more ideas as to how to rearrange the different parts, what to remove, what to add, what to replace, etc.

As you go about your day, look at everyday products and think about how you might improve them.

Improving Services

A service might have been designed in a way that made it less user-friendly or more complicated than it needed to be. In that case, you want to identify which parts of the service are not working well and remove them to make the service simpler and more user-friendly.

Sometimes services are lacking in something, and users can benefit from enhancing the service. An example is the return service used by retail shops. When e-commerce started, return services were quite rigid and didn't provide many options for customers. As e-commerce grew, the return service received a lot of attention from customers and businesses alike. Companies realised they needed to change their return service to make it easier for their customers to use.

The return service process can be broken down into these smaller elements:

- the customer's reason for returning an item,
- the customer's cost of returning an item,
- how a customer can return an item,
- where the customer can return an item,

- how much time the customer has from purchasing an item to be able to return it,
- the environmental impact of returning items.

When a service is broken down into its elements, it's easier to see which parts are working well, which parts need improvement, and which parts are not working at all or not required.

For example, retailers looked closely into the element of customer's cost of returning an item and realised the cost of returning an item drove some customers' buying decisions. If it costs money to return an item, people won't purchase items as frequently from this e-store. As a result, some stores have changed the cost of returning an item to zero.

In another example, stores realised their customers weren't happy with the environmental impact of returning items, and therefore made changes to ensure that the return process was more sustainable.

Exercise 19: Improving—A restaurant service

Use your creative thinking to improve the process of eating out at a restaurant. Think about everything that happens from the moment you reach the restaurant until you leave.

Answer these questions:

- What are the different parts of this service?
- What would happen if I removed a part?
- What would happen if I rearranged the parts?
- Can I simplify it?
- Can I add extra features?
- What is non-essential or unnecessary?

Exercise 20: Improving—Going to the cinema

Use your creative thinking and improve the experience of going to the cinema. Think about everything that happens from the time you purchase a ticket until you finish watching the movie and leave. Answer these questions:

- What are the different parts and elements of this process?
- What would happen if I removed a part?
- What would happen if I rearranged the parts?
- What can I substitute to make an Improvement?
- What can I make bigger or smaller?
- Can I add extra features?
- How can I simplify it?
- What is non-essential or unnecessary?

Let your imagination run wild and think of different ways to improve this experience.

Don't judge the ideas. Just let them flow and build on them.

Be creative with your thinking and try to come up with some crazy ideas.

Improving Ideas and Concepts

In addition to products and services, you can also improve ideas and concepts. By exploring what can be added, changed, removed, increased, or decreased from a concept, you can see how you can rearrange and redesign concepts to improve them.

For example, let's look again at the DVD rental service. In the '90s, DVD rental stores dominated the home entertainment market. Customers would rent a DVD from the store and pay late return fees if they didn't return it on time.

Reed Hastings and Marc Rudolph were frustrated with the concept of renting a DVD in-store and having to pay high late fees. So, they came up with a new concept for DVD rental that was renting DVDs by mail. This is how Netflix started.

After some time of using this concept, it became time to explore how to improve it. Reed and Marc improved this concept by also offering a subscription. Instead of paying for each individual DVD, customers could choose to have a subscription and pay a fixed monthly fee to rent as many DVDs as they wanted.

Another example for improving a concept relates to cash withdrawal through an ATM. For many years, the concept was that if you wanted to withdraw cash through an ATM, you had to use your bank card to do so. Commonwealth Bank of Australia decided to improve this concept by introducing a cardless cash option. This meant that customers could now also withdraw money from an ATM using their mobile phone, instead of using their bank card.

It is important to understand that we have the power to improve and change anything, even ideas and concepts that we may have grown up with and thought to be "fixed."

Exercise 21: Improving— Education

Use your creative thinking and improve the concept of the education system (mandatory system of school for children). Answer these questions:

- What is the purpose of schools? What are the goals?
- What should be the outcome of attending school for the students?
- How can I make it better?
- What needs to be changed?
- What is irrelevant?

- How can I simplify it?

What is non-essential or unnecessary?

How can I substitute the time, people, place, or materials?

Let your imagination run wild and think of new ways to design the education system. Break free from what exists today; break free from the status quo. Try to come up with some crazy and unusual ideas.

Exercise 22: Improving—Measuring a country's economic health

Today the most common way to measure a country's economic health is the GDP (Gross Domestic Product). But what exactly is measured? Answer these questions:

- What is the definition of economic success? Is there a need to change this definition?
- Are there other things that need to be measured?
- Are there things that don't need to be measured?
- How can I simplify it?
- What is non-essential or unnecessary?
- What can I substitute to make an Improvement?
- What can I remove? What can I add?
- What can I rearrange?
- What is irrelevant?
- What needs to be bigger or smaller?
- Is there a better way to measure a country's economic health?

Let your imagination run wild and think of new ways to measure a country's economic health. Don't judge the ideas. Just let them flow and build on them. Try to come up with some crazy ideas. The more ideas, the better.

Chapter Summary

- Improving means looking at the different components of a product, service, process, or concept and exploring how these different parts can be rearranged, replaced, changed, or removed to make it better and provide more value.
- Improving is about breaking free from *This is how it has always been done*, *This is how it is built*, and *This is how people use it*.
- Improving means moving away from what already exists and imagining *What if…?*
- To stay relevant and provide value, apply constant improvements.
- You can practise Improving with everyday products and processes that you may use.

Reflective Questions

Now that you are aware of Improving as a way to develop your imagination, creative thinking, and innovative problem-solving, it's time to incorporate Improving into your daily life.

Take this opportunity to reflect on the following questions:

1. How might you incorporate Improving as part of your problem-solving process?

   _____
   _____
   _____

2. How might you help your child develop Improving as a way of thinking?

   _____
   _____
   _____

3. How might you develop your own thinking using Improving as an innovative way of thinking?

   _____
   _____
   _____

CHAPTER 15:

WHAT IF...? — IMAGINING NEW WAYS

> "If you want something new, you have to stop doing something old."
> - Peter F. Drucker, Austrian management consultant, educator, and author

---

This chapter focuses on
- What it means to Imagine New Ways
- How Imagining New Ways is different from Repurposing, Merging, and Improving
- How to develop your Imaginative superpowers

Imagining New Ways is about looking at a process, service, policy, theory, way of thinking; articulating the concept behind it, and then looking for new ways to go about carrying out this concept. It's about breaking free from thinking *This is how we perceive this thing, This is how we approach it,* or *This is how we think about it.* When thinking big, Imagining New Ways is about breaking free from an existing concept and reimagining a new concept altogether.

Imagining New Ways is more appropriate for teenagers than younger children due to the complexity of thinking involved. However, for certain gifted younger children, the exercises in this chapter can stretch their thinking skills.

From Linear to Circular Economy

An example of Imagining New Ways is the shift from the concept of a linear economy to that of a circular economy. A linear economy is about taking raw materials, creating a product, using this product, and then throwing it away once there is no more use for it.

The linear economy creates a lot of waste. Waste is created during the different steps of the process, such as sourcing raw materials, transporting the materials, producing the products, packaging the products, and transporting the products. When the product reaches its end of life, more waste is produced by throwing it away.

The concept behind a linear economy is one of single-use. There is no regard for waste and the impact of this economy on our resources and environment in a linear economy. We all embrace the linear economy concept to create waste and pollution when we use disposable coffee cups, car tyres, single-use plastic bags, and many more products.

In contrast, a circular economy is about Imagining New Ways to approach how we manufacture and consume products and what happens to these products once they reach their end of life.

The circular economy concept means applying different methods such as reuse, sharing, repairing, and recycling to create a closed-loop system that reduces the generation of waste and pollution and maximises the use of our resources.

Looking at the Big Picture

As opposed to the previous types of *What if...?* thinking—Repurposing, Merging and Improving, Imagining New Ways is not about changing a physical product you use. It's instead about taking a step back and looking at the bigger picture, at the current way of thinking, and then moving away from that perception and approach. It's about moving away from the status quo.

For example, let's look at the taxi service. What is the concept behind taxis? Basically, a taxi service allows you to hire a driver with a car to take you from point A to point B.

In 2009, Garrett Camp and his friends were at a conference in Paris. They needed to get somewhere else, so they went outside in the windy and rainy weather to hail a cab. They stood outside for a long time in the stormy weather but couldn't get a cab to stop for them. This made Garrett think about how taxi services work and what he needed to do to get a cab. He thought to himself, *What if you could request a ride right from your mobile phone?* He developed an idea for connecting riders with local drivers, and he came up with what we know today as Uber[1].

Another example of breaking free of the status quo and finding new ways relates to home entertainment. TV began with the concept of broadcasting the same show to many TV sets. Do you remember the days you had to check the TV guide to know when the shows you wanted to watch would be on? Do you remember the days when you had to record a show if you were out at the broadcasting time? For many years, we all consumed home entertainment in this manner, and all media providers followed the same broadcasting concept.

Home entertainment today looks very different thanks to Netflix having imagined a new way to go about it. They came up with a radical idea: What if anyone could watch whatever TV show they wanted whenever they wanted to watch it? No TV guide. No schedule you need to follow. What if instead of broadcasting the same TV show to many TV sets, the customer could choose what they want to watch and have it streamed, on-demand, to their specific TV set?

With its new concept, Netflix disrupted the television industry, forced cable companies to change the way they do business, and transformed the entire telecom industry.

When you look at a concept and try to find new ways for that concept to be used, you steer away from what already exists and open your imagination to what can be.

 Here are a few questions to think about when Imagining New Ways:

1. What is the basic concept of this service, policy, or process? Strip it down to the basic idea.
2. Who uses this service, policy, or process? Who is providing the service, and who is consuming it?
3. Can someone else provide this service? Is there a different way to provide this service? Is there a different way to consume this service?
4. What are the problems, issues, and pain points of the current approach? How might I remove these problems, issues, and pain points?
5. What are the current limitations? What if I remove these limitations?
6. What are the current assumptions? What if I remove these assumptions?
7. Who is controlling the process? What if someone else controls it? What if no one controls it?

Imagining New Ways for Services

Exercise 23: Imagining New Ways—Electricity service

Let's look now at the concept of electricity service.

To consume electricity today, people have to use the services of a company that provides electricity. Many households today generate electricity through solar panels. However, they still need to use an electricity service provider to sell excess produced energy or consume energy when their solar panels can't produce enough energy to meet their energy needs.

Answer these questions:

- What is the basic concept behind electricity service providers?
- Can someone else provide this service? Is there a different way to provide this service? Is there a different way to consume this service?
- What are the current limitations? What if I remove these limitations?
- What are the current assumptions? What if I remove these assumptions?
- Who is currently controlling this process? What if someone else controls it? What if no one controls it?

Let your imagination run wild and think of different ways this concept might work.

Then take it further. Break free from the status quo. Think big and come up with a new concept.

Exercise 24: Imagining New Ways—Reactive, conventional medicine

In the Western world, conventional medicine is mainly focused on being reactive to symptoms and problems. People go to see a doctor when they don't feel well.

Answer these questions:

- What is the concept of a health system?
- What are the objectives of a health system, and how can these objectives be realised?
- What are the problems, issues, and pain points of the current approach? How might I remove these problems, issues, and pain points?
- What are the current limitations? What if I remove these limitations?
- What are the current assumptions? What if I remove these assumptions?

Let your imagination run wild and think of different ways to approach it. Go beyond the current way health systems operate. Try to come up with radical and crazy ideas. Don't judge the ideas. Just let them flow and build on these ideas.

Imagining New Ideas and Concepts

Exercise 25: Imagining New Ways—Owning a home

Let's look at the concept behind owning a home. Around the world, homeownership is perceived as a goal, something you need to work towards. In some countries, the percentage of homeownership is around 90 per cent. Romania is leading with almost 96 per cent of the population owning their homes, and many other countries are not far behind[2].

Owning your own home is a concept most of us grow up with and accept as a way of living. Owning your own home brings with it many benefits; however, it also brings with it a big mortgage, often requiring people to work their entire lives just to pay off the mortgage. This can impact your freedom to choose how to live your life. Answer these questions:

- What is the concept behind owning a home?
- What are the problems, issues, and pain points of the current approach? How might I remove these problems, issues, and pain points?
- What are the current limitations? What if I remove these limitations?
- What are the current assumptions? What if I remove these assumptions?

Let your imagination run wild and think of different ways to approach this idea. Go beyond the current status quo and the beliefs you grew up with. Try to come up with radical and crazy ideas. Don't judge the ideas. Just let them flow and build on these ideas.

Exercise 26: Imagining New Ways—Owning a car

Let's look at the concept behind owning a car. The mass production of cars, which started at the beginning of the twentieth century, triggered a love affair between humans and cars. It seems that everyone wants to own a car. Data on car ownership of Australian households in 2016 shows that 84.4 per cent of the households owned at least one car[3].

But why do we want to own a car? What is the concept behind owning a car? If we put aside owning a car as a status symbol, the concept of owning a car is to be able to get places (assuming it is feasible to drive there), whenever you want to do so. Owning a car means you always have access to a comfortable transportation mechanism that can also carry your shopping or what you need for a holiday.

Answer these questions:

- What are the problems, issues, and pain points of the current approach? How might I remove these problems, issues, and pain points?
- Is there a different way to go about this concept?

Go beyond what exists now and into new possibilities. Into new futures. Think creatively and come up with wild ideas.

Chapter Summary

- Imagining New Ways means looking at the core concept of a service, process, or policy and seeing it from a different angle.
- Imagining New Ways is about breaking free from *This is how we perceive this thing, This is how we approach it,* and *This is how we think about it.* It's about moving away from the status quo.
- Imagining New Ways can lead to an impactful, large-scale transformation when you start thinking big and imagining new concepts.

Reflective Questions

Now that you are aware of Imagining New Ways as a way to develop your imagination, creative thinking, and innovative mindset, it's time to incorporate this concept into your daily life.

Take this opportunity to reflect on the following questions:

1. How might you incorporate Imagining New Ways as part of your problem-solving process?

   _____
   _____
   _____

2. How might you help your child develop Imagining New Ways as a way of thinking?

   _____
   _____
   _____

3. How might you develop your own thinking through Imagining New Ways as an innovative way of thinking?

   _____
   _____
   _____

Final Note

You have come a long way on your journey, and I'm so proud of you! I'm sure you had challenges along the way, and it wasn't always smooth sailing, but you kept going.

By following this guide, adopting the mindset, and using the methods in this book, you have transformed yourself and created a wonderful innovative environment within your home. As a result, you are setting up your child for success in the twenty-first century and helping them become resilient, confident, independent thinkers, who can find innovative solutions to any problem.

You are a positive force, an innovation parent. Thanks to you, your child will be prepared to handle and thrive in the world, with all its complexities, uncertainties, and constant changes.

You have grown personally and professionally through reading and implementing the *Think Unique* approach and tools, but I want you to know that this is a lifelong journey. I have lived and breathed creative thinking, innovation, and design thinking every day for many years now, yet I still see myself as a student. I'm still only at the beginning, and I have so much more to learn. This is in part because I always believe I have a lot to learn from anyone and any scenario or environment I operate in. And partly because I know that in cultivating a lifelong student mindset, I keep my curiosity and "fresh eyes" mindset.

Although you've now reached the end of this book, I hope you'll keep it close to you and refer to it, to continue your growth and help the people you care for go on this journey as well. Often when you read something for the second, third, and fourth time, you discover new things in the text. You begin to understand it on a deeper level. When reading again, you can discover additional layers that you couldn't have seen before, as you were in a different place, with a different mindset, and different experiences.

Keeping in Touch—Continued Support

I want you to know that I am still here for you and will continue to support you on your journey. I encourage you to contact me and share with me your success stories and difficulties; let me know how I can further empower you as a parent. So, let's start a conversation: ortal@glitteringminds.com.au.

Reviews help authors more than you might think. If you enjoyed *Think Unique*, please consider leaving a review – I would greatly appreciate it.

Think Unique comes with resources you can download from https://www.glitteringminds.com.au/resources

And of course, make sure you stay in touch with me and Glittering Minds via your preferred social media channels. You can find us at:

- Facebook: https://www.facebook.com/ortal.green.79
- LinkedIn: https://au.linkedin.com/in/ortal-green-56857073
  https://au.linkedin.com/company/glittering-minds

I look forward to hearing from you!

Special People

Writing this book has been a journey of discovery.

Like any other journey, this journey had its ups and downs, its happy moments, and difficult times. I can honestly say that I couldn't have done it without the help and support of very special people. Therefore, I want to take this opportunity to say thank you to all the fantastic people in my life.

I want to especially thank the love of my life, Robby Green. Thank you for always going along with my crazy ideas and supporting all my adventures, no matter how mad they seem. Knowing you are always here for me helps me dream big and jump off cliffs while trusting it will be okay and that we will figure it all out on the way down. I know that together we can achieve anything we set our minds to.

Bonus – More Ideas on How to Develop Your Creativity

There are many ways to develop your and your child's creativity. Here are a few more ideas and tips on how you can become more creative.

1. **Learn new things.** As adults, we often read and learn only about things that are related to our occupation. If you focus only on developing yourself within your profession, you won't spend time exploring topics beyond your work. By doing so, you close your mind to new and wonderful worlds and to cross-pollination that will better your thinking. The more knowledge you have, not only in-depth but in breadth, the more your brain will be able to create connections between different things and come up with better ideas. An easy way to learn new things is to take an interest in other people who work in different professions. Ask them questions about what they do. Explore the reason behind different tasks they perform at work. Be curious about others and learn about how others live their personal and professional lives.
2. **Break your habits.** The brain is a lazy organ. Whenever it can, it will go on autopilot. The brain switches to autopilot when it knows what to do, as it has done it many times in the past. For example, if you drive on the same road to work, go to the same coffee shop, and do the same things all the time, you will stop noticing things. Your mind will not interact in a meaningful way with the environment around you. You need to break your habits so your brain will be present. When you are in a new environment, doing something new, your brain is alert, and you notice new things, hear new sounds, and pay

attention to the behaviours of other people. Therefore, to make sure your mind is more present and absorbs new information, get into the habit of breaking your habits. Try new things regularly.

3. **Change the scale at which you look at things.** Zoom in and zoom out. Sometimes you look at a problem or event from a close angle. This means you are missing related things that are a bit further away. It means you are narrowing your view and understating, as you can't see the big picture. When this happens, you need to zoom out and look at the problem from different distances. And sometimes, you are so far away, looking at the problem from such a remote distance, that you miss very important aspects of the problem. It is important to keep zooming in and out. Looking at the problem from different distances will enable you to understand it better.

4. **Keep a journal of your ideas.** But don't just leave it there and never lay your eyes again on what you wrote. Refer to your previous ideas from time to time. Going over your previous ideas might help you generate more ideas or help you with a particular problem you are exploring at the moment.

5. **Get out of your comfort zone.** Do things that scare you. Open yourself up to completely new experiences. For example, if the thought of public speaking makes you break into a sweat, take a public speaking course. If you always need to be in control, and you're afraid to just let go and trust that everything will be okay, try sky diving. If you've never tried dancing before, then take a dance class.

6. **Have conversations with people you wouldn't normally engage with.** Have chats with strangers. Whether it is the cashier at the supermarket, the Uber driver, a person on the train, someone at work you've never spoken with, or the receptionist at an office building. Ask them how they are doing and get to know their perspective. Don't forget to smile.

7. **Be brave with the clothes and colours you are wearing.** Most of us have some type of clothes we would never dare

to wear or some colours we steer clear of. Do something different. If you've never worn a pink shirt, go for it. If you've never worn a tie with crazy colours and cartoons on it, do it.

8. **Imagine stories.** Develop your creativity and imagination by creating stories on the spot. Improvise other people's stories in real-time. One way to go about it is turning on your TV, choose any channel or anything to stream, and then turn off the volume. Now narrate what is going on. Try to go wild with your imagination. What are the characters saying? Allow yourself to be silly. Have fun with your imagination and create any script you want. Another way to go about it is to go out to a restaurant, bar, or coffee shop and look at the people sitting around you. What is their story? Create a story for them. What are they saying to each other? What are their dreams and hopes? What are their struggles and difficulties? Create a detailed story about them.

9. **Look at nature.** Explore natural ecosystems, evolution processes, and different animals and their attributes and behaviours. Look at microorganisms, space, stars, and other planets. Explore what happens deep in our oceans and learn about marine life. Learning about nature will enrich your knowledge and help you find new connections between how nature operates and the problems you explore. Often, answers and ideas are found in nature.

A Deep Dive into RIDER

I wrote this section for parents interested in deeper dive into the creative thinking process in action. If you want to see the RIDER process in a more structured way, for any educational setup, this section is for you. (This is a deeper dive into the example you saw in chapter 9.)

Applying the Creative Thinking Process

To start, you'll need to choose the project question you and your child will work on. It's important to choose a question your child can relate to. It needs to be relevant for them, impacts them, a question they care about, and something they feel invested in.

When children (and adults) feel connected to what they are working on, they are more engaged and make more of an effort. Engaged children learn better and also behave better.

Choosing the right question for children to work on can empower them to drive change and become caring, participating members of their communities.

So, what question should we choose to use in this example?

Let's see the creative process in action while working on an important, real-world question related to something very close to our hearts-our family.

I believe the importance of spending time as a family won't come as a surprise to you.

We all know there are many benefits to spending time with our loved ones. Furthermore, this time together as a family is crucial for our children's development and wellbeing.

Children who grow up in families that spend time together:

- are less stressed
- are more resilient
- are more confident
- have better mental health
- perform better academically
- have fewer behavioural issues
- are better at dealing with conflicts

The benefits of spending time as a family are not limited to our kids. Parents benefit greatly from spending time with their families too.

Spending time with your loved ones develops special bonds between family members and creates trust and beautiful memories.

With all these fantastic benefits you would think that we will make sure to spend a lot of time with each other. While this might be our desire, what we wish for our family and how we want to live our lives, the reality is sometimes quite different.

A study performed by Visit Anaheim on the time families spend together found that families spend only 37 minutes of quality time together per day. Just 37 minutes!

There are a few significant reasons for this decline. Our lives are becoming more and more hectic, with parents:

- working more hours
- experiencing more stress
- handling packed kids' activities schedules

And with the non-stop presence of technology in our lives that creates constant interruptions, we spend less and less time as a family.

If you raised your eyebrow now, wondering if your family enjoys more than 37 minutes of quality time together per day, there is something you need to be aware of. We often confuse the time we spend on screens while our family members are around as family time.

Research performed by Killian Mullan from Oxford University and Stella Chatzitheochari from the University of Warwick found that we spend more alone time together.

As it turns out, families spend *more* time together than ever before. But it is not a together-together time. It is more of an alone-together time.

This alone-together time means that although our family members are at home together more than before, we spend this time doing activities on our own. Therefore, it is actually alone time and not family quality time.

You probably guessed correctly that a lot of this alone-together time is taken up by screens.

The good news is we can change it. If we want to strengthen our family relationships, cultivate our wellbeing, and have fun as a family, we can make it happen. Therefore, our project question would be –

How might we spend more time as a family?

Throughout this example, I've done my best to provide a detailed explanation for how solving problems using the creative process can look in a home environment. As there are significant differences between children's capabilities, depending on their age and other factors, I leave it to you, the parent, to try out and decide what works best with your child. Feel free to dial it up or down as you see fit for your own child.

So, where do we start? As per our acronym RIDER, the starting point is the first stage of the creative process, **R**esearch.

Step 1: Research—The Starting Point

To perform thorough research, we need to start by exploring the question itself. In our example, *How might we spend more time as a family?* We need to start by understanding why it is an important question to explore.

When introducing this question to your child, ask them why is it important to spend time as a family? Discuss it with your child.

Explore with your child the benefits of spending time together as a family. You can start this exploration as a discussion and then search online. While exploring together, you can ask your child these questions-

- What type of activities do you like to do as a family? Why?
- What might prevent us from spending time together?
- Describe the best day with our family. What are we doing together that makes it so special?
- What makes you happy? Why?
- What makes you feel loved?

Once you and your child feel you have a good understanding of the importance of this project question, ask your child if you need to involve other people in exploring *How might we spend more time as a family?*

When working on a problem, it is essential to involve everyone related to this problem or question in finding a solution.

In this case, it means involving all family members.

Planning the Interview

A great way to understand the different family members views on our question is by interviewing them. But before you can interview people, you need to plan the interview questions you'll be asking. Consider the following:

1. What are the objectives of this interview? What are you hoping to understand and learn from the interview?
2. What are the questions you need to ask to help you achieve your objectives?

This is a good exercise to do with your child. It will be an opportunity to talk about the need to think of and set up objectives and goals for a task you want to perform. You need to understand what outcomes you want to achieve before beginning an activity. (Planning always sets you up for a good start.)

For our project question, the interview objectives for the family members might be to understand:

1. What might prevent us from spending more time together,
2. What kind of activities we like to do as a family,
3. How might we spend more quality time as a family.

Kinds of Questions to Ask in the Interview

Once everyone is clear on the objectives, ask your child to suggest the questions they will need to ask to achieve the goals you set up together.

When you write the questions for the interview with your child, be mindful of how you word these questions, as not all questions are equal. The way you word your questions impacts the results you get. Specific wording can lead the interviewee to provide a particular answer. To receive reliable data from the interview, the questions need to be unbiased and not leading.

So, let's look at a few tips to word questions well:

Tip #1: Open-ended vs closed-ended questions. There is a big difference between asking an open-ended and a closed-ended question, when it comes to the answers you get.

An open-ended question is one that invites detailed answers and elaborate explanations and provides the person you are asking with room to say what they think, how they feel, and what they experienced. They can express their point of view. These types of questions are suitable to use when you want to understand the other person, get more information, or explore a topic. Open-ended questions are used when you want to have a conversation, elicit more information, and have an open dialogue.

An example of an open-ended question is "What would be your ideal holiday?" Open-ended questions often start the following ways:

"Why…"

"What…"

"How…"

In contrast, a closed-ended question is one that usually invites a one-word answer—simply yes or no. You can think of a closed-ended question as a multiple-choice question where often there are only two choices, *yes* and *no*. This type of question is suitable to use when you need a clear answer to a question (black or white) or when you want to survey large groups of people and easily perform statistical analysis on the data. (In that case, you can write it as a multiple- choice question for which you provide answer options.) Closed-ended questions are used when you need a quick, short answer, and do not intend to create a conversation.

An example of a closed-ended question is: "Did you watch a movie last night?" Closed-ended questions often start with the following words:

"Did…"

"Do…"

"Have you…"

"Are…"

"Is…"

"Was…"

You can turn an open-ended question into a closed-ended question and vice versa. For example, "Do you like dogs?" can be turned into an open-ended question by changing it to "How do you feel about dogs?" This open-ended question, "How might being a parent impact your life?" can be changed into a closed-ended question by changing it to "Is being a parent impacting your life?"

Children need to understand the difference between closed-ended and open-ended questions and be mindful of the type of answer each one will bring. You can ask your child to explain the difference between an open-ended and a closed-ended question. Discuss it with them and ask them to provide examples for each type of question.

Explore with your child how the type of answers you get can change based on the type of questions you ask (one-word answer vs more detailed answer). You can use the two questions below to demonstrate the difference in the responses you receive for open-ended questions and closed-ended questions. Present the first question and ask your child to answer it. Then present the second question and ask them to answer it.

1. How do you feel about going on a road trip with your family?
2. Would you like to go on a road trip with your family?

Have a discussion with your child about when it's best to use a closed-ended question and an open-ended question.

Tip #2: Leading vs neutral questions. We often ask questions without being aware that the way we ask the question influences the answer we get. This kind of question is a *leading question,* and asking a leading question can result in getting a biased or false answer. For example, let's say you want to check how your child feels about completing a task you have given them. You can ask this question: "What was difficult about performing this task?"

This question has a hidden assumption that your child has struggled to perform the task. There is an expectation that this task has some elements that your child found difficult. Since you are asking this question with an assumption, your child will understand from the question that you expect them to have some difficulties with this task. This, in turn, can influence the answer you get and might lead to a biased or false answer.

You can remove this assumption by changing your question to "How was your experience working on this task?" This type of wording provides your child with the freedom to answer this question as per their experience. It gives them the freedom to reflect on the task and assess how they felt about completing it. It allows them to reflect on whether this task was easy or difficult. Neutrally framing this question enables your child to answer in a way true to how they experienced working on this task.

We all ask leading questions all the time, but we need to become mindful of it so we can word our questions as neutral ones.

Parents often ask their children, "Did you have a good day at school?" This question is both closed-ended, providing little room for a detailed answer, and leading. Within this question, there is the expectation to hear from the child that their day at school was good.

This question can be reframed as an open-ended and neutral question: "How was your day at school?" This way, the child is free to provide a detailed answer true to their real experience at school.

Here are a few more examples of how a question can be transformed from a leading question to a neutral one:

Biased/Leading question	Unbiased/Neutral question
Was it a good movie?	What do you think about this movie?
Why are you so upset?	How do you feel?
Why do you not care about using plastic bags?	How do you feel about using plastic bags?

Have a discussion with your child about leading questions. Try out using leading and neutral questions with them to see the difference in the answers you receive.

If you want to ask about a specific feeling or experience but want to avoid leading with your question, there is something you can do about it. You can use the mighty word "might," to remove assumptions from your question.

For example, let's say you want to understand what makes your child feel upset at school. You can word it as a leading question: What makes you feel upset at school? (This question has an assumption that your child feels upset when they are at school.) Or you can add the word "might," which removes this assumption: What might make you feel upset at school?

Adding the word "might" means the question is not leading as you still provide your child with the freedom to answer that nothing makes them feel upset at school.

Setting the Interview Questions

Let's return now to planning the family members interview questions. As mentioned earlier, this is what we want to understand from performing these interviews: (The interview objectives)

- What might prevent us from spending more time together,
- What kind of activities we like to do as a family,
- How might we spend more quality time as a family.

Here are some examples of interview questions:

1. Once you finish work or school, what activities do you do until you go to sleep? How much time, roughly, do you spend on each activity? (Include activities such as time on social media platforms, phone calls with different people, time spent on hobbies, reading books, any errands that you run etc.)
2. What type of activities do you do during weekends? How much time, roughly, do you spend on each activity? (Include activities such as time on social media platforms, phone calls with different people, time spent on hobbies, reading books, any errands that you run etc.)
3. Thinking about the previously mentioned activities, what can you do differently to allow for more family quality time? (A quality time together is a time where you interact with each other, paying full attention to each other, without any distractions. Watching a movie together is not considered quality time together, and neither is eating together when everyone is on their phones)
4. What type of activities do you wish to do with our family? Why?
5. Thinking about our family, what might come in the way of us spending more quality time together?
6. As a family, what do we need to do differently to have more time together during weekdays?
7. As a family, what do we need to do differently to have more time together during weekends?

Preparing to Interview

It is essential to prepare your child on how to perform interviews. The first thing they need to realise is that they interview others to understand their world. To understand how things look from their perspective. (The same apply to anytime you ask someone a question.)

Therefore, when your child interviews your family members, they need to keep an open mind, remove any judgment and accept that different people have different opinions. There is no right and wrong point of view, only a difference of perspective.

In addition, to get the most out of an interview, your child needs to follow these guidelines:

1. Explain to the interviewee why they want to interview the person. (For example, "This interview will help me gain a better understanding of how we can spend more quality time as a family.")
2. Ask the interviewee to be honest and share their thoughts and opinions. Explain that there is no right or wrong answer.
3. Encourage the interviewee to provide detailed answers. (More information gathered through the interviews means a better understanding of the topic you are researching.)

At the end of the interview, they can thank the person they interviewed for their time and input.

Looking for Inspiration Elsewhere

Another thing that you can do with your child during your research phase is look for inspiration elsewhere. What do other families do to allow more quality time together? What information can you find online on spending quality time as a family?

Making Sense of Your Data

Once you and your child have finished with your research, it's time to look at all the data you've collected and start to investigate what it means. It is time to make sense of it. So, let's break down this process into manageable steps.

The first step is to analyse the data from the interviews. To do so, your child needs to take one interviewee's answer sheet and write the answer for each question on separate Post-It notes.

But it is not as straightforward as just copying the answer to a Post-It note.

One answer can include a few separate pieces of information. For example, for the question "Once you finish work or school, what activities do you do until you go to sleep?" an answer can be, "I prepare dinner for about one hour, I watch TV for about 3 hours, I eat dinner for about 30 minutes, I spend one hour on Facebook."

This answer includes four different pieces of information about the activities this person does. When transcribing this answer onto Post-It notes, each piece of information will need to be copied to a different note, as per the below:

1. The first Post-It note will say, "Prepare dinner – one hour".
2. The second Post-It note will say, "Watch TV – 3 hours".
3. The third Post-It note will say, "Eating dinner – half an hour".
4. The fourth Post-It note will say, "Facebook – one hour".

Then, place together all the Post-It notes with the answers to the same questions.

Here is an example of how transcribing all the answers for an interview question looks:

You will end up with very colourful walls!

Now that you have all the answers to the same question together, explain to your child how to identify similar answers. Use one of the interview questions and answers as an example. Pick up two Post-It notes, read them out loud, and ask your child if these answers are similar.

You'll find that interesting discussion emerge from this activity. You and your child may disagree on what is similar and what is not.

Therefore, it's an excellent opportunity to practice dealing with and resolving differences of opinion.

Once you agree on which answers are similar, they need to be grouped. This activity of grouping together continues until your child has gone over all the answers to the question.

It might be that some Post-It notes (answers) will be alone, as there won't be any similar answers. This is to be expected.

For each question, your child grouped the answers for, ask them to name the theme of the three biggest answer groups (groups with the most similar responses). The name needs to capture the essence of this answer group.

This is an example of how answers to one interview question are grouped:

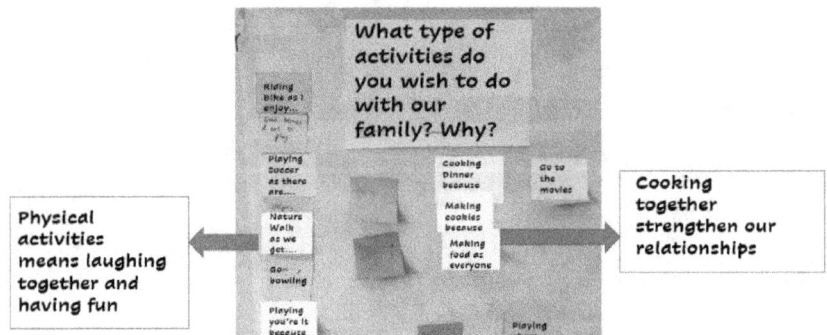

Ask your child to write down the themes for each interview question, as per the below example. (Summarise it in a document that you and your child can refer to later on.)

1. Once you finish work or school, what activities do you do until you go to sleep?

- We are watching TV/YouTube for over 2 hours.
- We are spending more than 2 hours on social media.
- We are eating dinner for about 30 minutes.

2. What type of activities do you do during weekends?

- We like to spend time with our friends for about 4 hours.
- House maintenance keeps us busy for around 4 hours.
- We enjoy family fun activities for about 2 hours.

3. What type of activities do you wish to do with our family? Why?

- Cooking together strengthen our relationships.
- Physical activities means laughing and having fun.
- Playing cards and board games creates a great bond and memories.

This is how you and your child understand the meaning of the data you have gathered and come up with insights and new understandings.

Summarise your insights from other activities performed as part of the research phase.

Presenting the Results

You and your child can place all the insights from the research stage on one of the walls at your home. The headline for this wall should be the question you are working on: "How might we spend more time as a family?"

 You can use this project as an opportunity to introduce and practise using graphs to present and understand research data. Have a conversation with your child on choosing which type of graph to use to present research data.

Here are two examples of how you and your child can present the results of your research, with each example using a different question from the interview. (You and your child can use PowerPoint or a spreadsheet to create graphs).

The first example uses the question, "Once you finish work or school, what activities do you do until you go to sleep?"

After grouping the different answers, your child can use a pie chart to present the family members' activities after school/work.

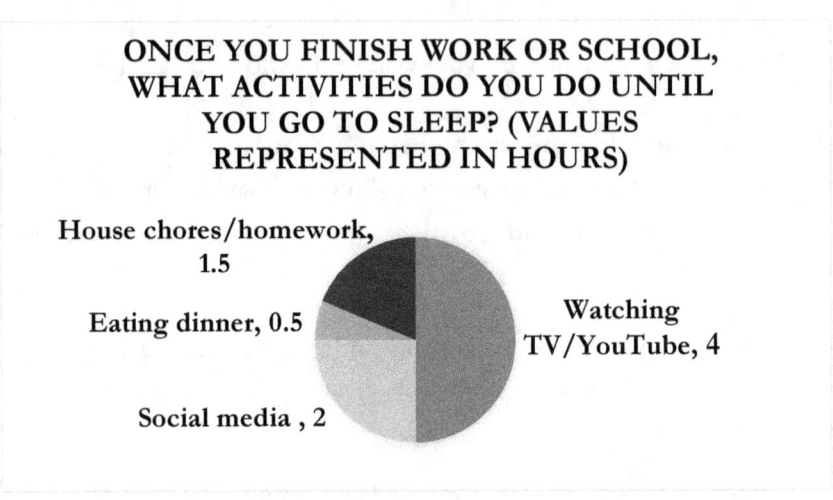

Below is the second example. In this example, the question used is "What type of activities do you enjoy doing with our family?"

Here we use a bar chart to represent the popularity of the different themes. The size of each theme is the number of Post-It notes within that theme.

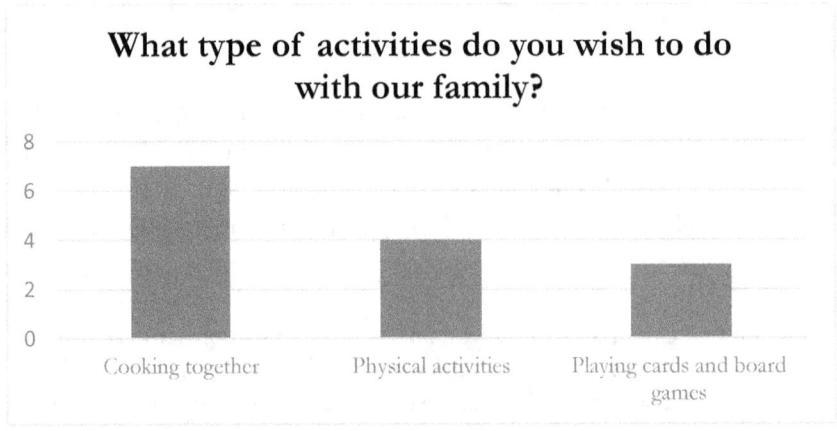

Skills Being Developed

When performing the **R**esearch stage in this manner, your child develops the following skills:

- Understanding the differences between open-ended and closed- ended questions
- Understanding the differences between leading and neutral questions
- Able to define objectives and desired outcomes for a task
- Able to interview and prepare interview questions
- How to plan and perform in-depth research
- How to perform data analysis and synthesis
- How to resolve conflicts arising from differences of opinion
- Empathy
- Curiosity
- Collaboration
- Verbal communication
- How to use graphs to present data

Step 2: Incubate—Allow Time to Digest

At this stage in the creative process, your child has a chance to reflect on insights and connect different pieces of information in their brains. Teachers and parents I've worked with have found that they need to give children time to ponder a question; they can't expect children to come up with answers right away. These parents are now aware that children will need time to digest a question, a period of incubation, and that some allowance for time to reflect needs to be part of the process.

As preparation for the incubation stage, you need to first frame your project question by using your new understandings and insights from the research performed. Here is an example for framing:

> **Question statement:** How might we spend more time as a family?
>
> **Target audience:** Our family members.
>
> **Needs:** To have time where all family members are relaxed, fully participating, having conversations and having fun together.
>
> **Difficulties:** Getting caught up in our busy day to day life, getting "sucked" into social media, being tired after a day at work, having too many errands and chores during weekends.

Target audience – These are the people involved in your project question.

Needs – These are the needs discovered by performing data analysis and synthesis on the interview data.

Difficulties - These are the difficulties discovered by performing data analysis and synthesis on the interview data.

You and your child can write the framing of your project's question on a big piece of paper and hang it on a wall. Now that everyone is clear on the problem and the understanding and insights from the research, it's time to spark your child' creativity.

Researchers have found one simple way to do this, and that is for your child to take a break from thinking about the problem. People who take a break, or incubate, can come up with not only more ideas but also more unique ideas than people who don't take a break.

Further, the type of activity you perform during your incubating time influences the effectiveness of this break on your creativity. There are three types of breaks you can take:

1. Break with no specific task to perform.
2. Break with an undemanding task for your brain.
3. Break with a demanding task for your brain.

As the research shows, people who performed an undemanding task during the incubation period outperformed those who did the demanding task or no task at all. This is because when you take a break without performing any tasks, your conscious mind is still contemplating the original problem you want to solve. When you take a break by doing a demanding task for your brain, your brain needs to focus on performing that task. This, in turn, prevents your brain from switching into an "idle" state that will enable your subconscious mind to think about your original problem.

To summarise, for a time of incubation to have a positive impact on creative thinking, your conscious mind needs to work on an undemanding task during a break, while your subconscious mind works on creating new connections to solve the problem or question you are exploring.

Let's look now at the length of the incubation time. The incubating period depends on the complexity of the problem. The more complex the problem is, the more time required for incubation. In terms of incubating time for your child, you'll want to allocate three to ten minutes for this activity.

In terms of what type of activity to choose for this purpose, it is best to select a task very different from your original problem. This undemanding task can be as simple as tidying up the house, building a tower from different materials, or going for a walk.

You can take time for incubation during the next stage, *Dream*, if you feel that your child has provided ideas and then got stuck. When they can't develop more ideas, a break with an undemanding task can help them generate new ideas.

When performing the Incubate stage in this manner, your child develops the following skills:

- Collaboration
- Verbal communication

- Ability to articulate a problem including the needs and difficulties of the target audience
- Empathy

Step 3: Dream—Brainstorm Ideas

This is the time to revisit your newly framed question and come up with ideas to help your target audience with their needs and difficulties. Children love coming up with ideas to solve a problem, even more so when it's a real-world problem that impacts them.

For your project question, it will be fantastic if all family members brainstorm ideas.

Go over the brainstorming rules with everyone as listed in Chapter 8 for Step 3, Dream, on page 118. (You can download these rules at www.glitteringminds.com.au/resources). As a facilitator, make sure everyone adheres to the rules, so there is a safe environment to express ideas.

Encourage your family members to build on each other's ideas and to let their imaginations run wild. As an example, here are a few ideas for solutions to the question, "How might we spend more time as a family?":

1. A few times a week cook dinner together.
2. Ban the use of mobile phones during dinner.
3. Make sure everyone eats dinner together.
4. Once a week have a board game night.
5. Go on a bike ride during weekends.
6. A few times a week go to the park together.
7. Have a "no screens" night once a week.
8. Rest when you get home after work.
9. Split the house chores between more family members.
10. Use deliveries instead of going to the shops.

 If your family members get stuck, or you feel their ideas are trivial and there is a need to dig deeper for more innovative ideas, you may want to take them further by introducing "crazy ideas" and letting them build on these ideas. For example:

1. Getting rid of all our screens.
2. Go on a family holiday every weekend.
3. Stop working.
4. Stop going to school.

With your help as a facilitator, let's see how your family members can take two of these crazy ideas and build on them.

Crazy idea #1: Go on a family holiday every weekend. The essence of this idea is that when we are on holiday, we don't spend time on chores and errands and have a lot of time as a family.

While it would be fantastic to go on a holiday every weekend, it is probably not a viable option financially. However, what we can do, is bring the holiday into our home. What I mean by that is that we can pretend we are on a holiday while staying at home. We can decide that we are not doing any chores and errands during this weekend. We can spend all of the time as a family, doing things together. We can even go camping in our living room, tell each other campfire stories while using a torchlight, and play cards.

Crazy idea #2: Stop working. The concept here is for parents to have more time with their family. For parents to free more space in their lives, to make their lives less busy and less tiring.

Here's how this concept can be applied: Check whether you can work less. There are different ways to reduce your working hours– reduce commute time, become more efficient, create clear boundaries between working time and home time, reduce your working hours etc.

If you simply feel tired after a day at work, think about what can re-energise you before you come home to your family and do it.

If you need to clear your mind from work to be fully present with your family, explore ways to disconnect from work while you are with your loved ones.

We now have these additional ideas to add to our list:

1. Have a holiday at home.
2. Create clear boundaries between work and home time.

When performing the **D**ream stage in this manner, your child develops the following skills:

- Collaboration
- Empathy
- Creative thinking
- Creative confidence
- Verbal communication
- How to brainstorm ideas

Step 4: Evaluate

Once the **D**ream stage is completed, it's time to evaluate the ideas.

Start by grouping similar ideas with your family members. This helps in reducing the number of ideas you will need to evaluate.

In this step, your family members will need to choose what criteria to use to rate their ideas.

Criteria for Rating Ideas

Your family members will need to choose a few criteria to rate their ideas against. For each question/problem you and your child are working on, you will need to consider what the most important or influential factors are for the success of this project and have those factors as the criteria for this step.

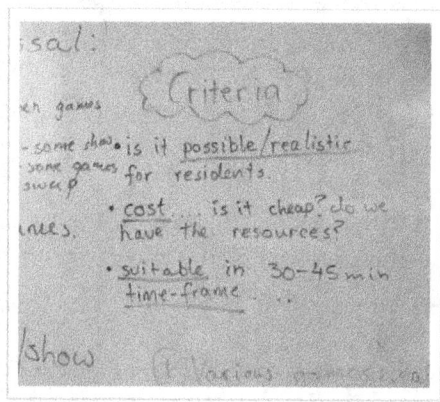
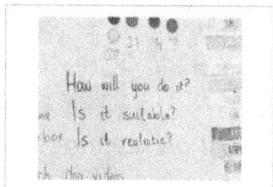
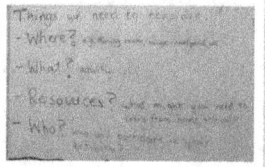

Discuss with your family members the practical aspects they need to consider to evaluate their ideas. Ask them to come up with what they need to consider to assess if an idea can be a successful solution. Ask them to explain the reasons behind their thinking.

 This is an opportunity for your child to practise their communication skills, critical-thinking, and verbal persuasion techniques.

For the project question we are working on, the criteria can be:

1. Can we really make it happen?
2. Will you agree to this? (Need to check if all family members will do it)
3. Will the outcome of doing this be more quality time as a family?

Once you decide as a family on the criteria, it is time to vote for each idea.

You will need to make a table with the ideas as the columns and the criteria as the rows. You can create this table on a spreadsheet or use paper.

Before voting, you can facilitate an open discussion where each family member shares how they evaluate an idea against the criterion. This is an opportunity for everyone to practise their communication and verbal persuasion techniques.

Once this discussion is finished, each will need to vote if they think the idea answers the specific criterion. (They vote for it if they think the answer to the criterion question is Yes.)

Let's see how this step would work when voting on four ideas:

Criteria	Ban the use of mobile phones during dinner	Split the house chores between more family members	A few times a week cook dinner together	Have a holiday at home
Can we really make it happen?	5 (5 family members voted yes)	3	5	5
Will you agree to this?	5	3	5	5
Will the outcome of doing this be more quality time as a family?	5	2	5	5
Total	15	8	15	15

Once the evaluation process is complete, your family will have a list of ideas with ratings for each one of them. You can then decide how many ideas you want to bring into Step 5, **R**ealise, and prototype them.

When performing the **E**valuation stage in this manner, your child develops the following skills:

- Collaboration
- Resilience
- Critical thinking
- Verbal persuasion
- Creative thinking
- Confidence
- Verbal communication
- How to come up with criteria and evaluate ideas

Step 5: Realise—Bring Ideas to Life

Now it's time to prototype the top ideas for solutions so your family members can provide feedback on them.

Let your child be creative in how they will **R**ealise the ideas. There is no right or wrong way. The main point is to have something they can share to help others understand the concept and enable others to imagine it, ask questions, and provide feedback.

To achieve this outcome, your child needs to create a *prototype*. A prototype is an early model of an idea for a product, service, or process that is not yet the finished version. People build prototypes to turn an idea into something tangible that can be tested. It's a great way to test a concept, learn from it, and refine your idea.

Here are a few ways to create a prototype and bring ideas to life:

1. Create a schematic drawing of the idea.
2. Create a visual presentation that explains how the idea works (using visual aids helps get across a message).
3. Create an advertisement to explain the idea.

4. Create a model.
5. Write a story (or comic strip) about your idea.
6. Create a role-play or skit about it.

 Ask your child first to plan their prototype. Ask them to think about what they want to create. It is good to get your child to think and plan before they embark on a task, as it sets them up for a good start.

For example, your child can prototype the idea of having a holiday at home. What is it going to look like? What will the family be doing during this home holiday?

Your child can create an ad for this holiday at home or draw what all of you will be doing.

Now that the prototypes are ready, it's time to involve others and get feedback. For your project, the right people to involve are your family members as these solutions impact them.

Preparing for Feedback

At this point, you'll want to prepare your child on how to present their prototypes and get meaningful feedback. This is an excellent time to have a deep discussion about the meaning of feedback.

Often, children (and adults too) see feedback as personal criticism, and therefore, for them, good feedback is only when someone tells you, "This is great!" But what can you learn from such feedback? How does it help you improve your creation? In truth, it doesn't.

Getting feedback is all about learning what is working well, what is not working, and where you need to improve. It's an opportunity to learn. Good feedback helps you improve and get better.

Discuss with your child the below questions:

1. What is feedback?
2. What is the purpose of providing and receiving feedback?
3. What kind of feedback is useful and helps us?

You're going to enjoy some interesting discussions around these questions. The point of such conversations is to help your child understand that getting constructive feedback is a good thing, and it doesn't reflect on them personally or on their capabilities and talents. It is important to learn to separate feedback from self-esteem. Gaining this understanding will help your child thrive throughout their entire life.

Working with the creative thinking process will help your child realise how feedback can help them learn and improve, and they will start seeking it.

Let's take a look at the questions your child is going to ask to elicit constructive feedback. At Glittering Minds, we have a standard feedback form we use. Sometimes we need to tweak it, depending on the specific project needs or the people who are providing the feedback. The basic questions are as follows:

1. What did you like about the prototype? (It's important to start on a positive note.)
2. What would you change? (This is an opportunity to have a discussion to learn more. This is where there is a need to ask many "why" questions and ask for elaboration on opinions and thoughts.)
3. Do you have any questions? (Asking this question allows you to understand whether something is not clear about the solution itself or whether there are gaps in the solution.)
4. Do you have any suggestions for improvements? (This is another opportunity to get ideas from the person who is testing the prototype. It might be that the previous questions and the time to digest and reflect on the solution helped in triggering more ideas for improvement.)

 Explain to your child that they first need to explain their prototype and how it works, and then ask the feedback questions. Remind your child to ask why and seek detailed answers (similar to interviewing).

After the prototype has been tested and feedback has been received, it is time to reflect on the feedback and decide on the next steps. Some questions to ask are:

1. Is this prototype a good solution for the problem? If it is not, it is time to move on to another idea.
2. Is there a need to make changes and improve the prototype?

If the prototype seems like a good solution but needs a few changes, now is the time to implement these changes. You can perform testing again after the improvements have been made to get additional feedback on the product. This is an iterative process that helps create a solution suitable and desirable by the users.

When performing the **R**ealise stage in this manner, your child develops the following skills:

- Collaboration
- Resilience

- Critical thinking
- Creative thinking
- Confidence
- Verbal communication
- Presentation
- How to seek feedback
- How to improve your product/idea based on feedback

Notes

Introduction

1. Concordia University St. Paul "Using Design Thinking in Mathematics for Middle School Students: A Multiple Case Study of Teacher Perspectives"
2. Hacettepe University "Design Thinking in Mathematics Education: The Minecraft Case"
3. North Carolina State University "Using Design Thinking to Create a New Education Paradigm for Elementary Level Children for Higher Student Engagement and Success"

Chapter 2

1. Sun, Jiangzhou, Quinlin Chen, Qinglin Zhang, et al. "Training your brain to be more creative: brain functional and structural changes induced by divergent thinking training," *Hum Brain Mapp.* (2016) 37(10):3375-3387. doi:10.1002/hbm.23246

Chapter 3

1. Del Rey, Jason. "How robots are transforming Amazon warehouse jobs – for better and worse," *Vox.* (December 11, 2019) http://www.vox.com/recode/2019/12/11/20982652/"https://www.vox.com/recode/2019/12/11/20982652/robots-amazon-warehouse-jobs-automation

2. Nam, DJu Gang, Sunggyun Park, Eui Jin Hwang, Jong Hyuk Lee, Kwang-Nam Jin, Kun Young Lim, Thienkai Huy Vu, Jae Ho Sohn, Sangheum Hwang, Jin Mo Goo, and Chang Min Park. *Development and Validation of Deep Learning—based Automatic Detection Algorithm for Malignant Pulmonary Nodules on Chest Radiographs*. Radiology (2019) 290:1, 218-228.
3. Haridy, Rich. "Is this art? AI-generated portrait fetched over $400,000 at auction," *New Atlas*. (October, 28, 2018) https://newatlas.com/ai-art-auction-obvious-belamy/56984/
4. Van Nuys, Amanda. "New *LinkedIn* Research: Upskill Your Employees with the Skills Companies Need Most in 2020," LinkedIn. (December 28, 2019) https://www.linkedin.com/business/learning/blog/learning-and-development/most-in- demand-skills-2020
5. PwC. "The talent challenge: Harnessing the power of human skills in the machine age," *PwC*. (accessed: May 6, 2020) https://www.pwc.com/gx/en/ceo-survey/2017/deep-dives/ceo- survey-global-talent.pdf
6. IBM Institute for Business Value. *Capitalizing on Complexity: Insights from the Global Chief Executive Officer Study*. Canada: Conference Board of Canada, 2010. https://www.ibm.com/downloads/cas/1VZV5X8J

Chapter 4

1. McSpadden, Kevin. "You Now Have a Shorter Attention Span Than a Goldfish," *Time Magazine*. (May 14, 2015) https://time.com/3858309/attention-spans-goldfish/

Chapter 5

1. Land, George, and Jarman Beth. *Breakpoint and Beyond: Mastering the Future Today.* (US: HarperCollins Publishers, 1992).
2. Zhao, Yong. "Flunking Innovation and Creativity," Phi Delta Kappan (September 2012) 94(1):56-61. University of Kansas. DOI:10.2307/41763573 https://www.researchgate.net/publication/262091653_Flunking_Innovation_and_Creativity

Chapter 6

1. "List of best-selling books," Wikipedia. (accessed: June 2020) https://en.wikipedia.org/wiki/List_of_best-selling_books

Chapter 7

1. Wnuk, Alexis. "How the Brain Changes with Age," *Brain Facts.* (August 30, 2019) https://www.brainfacts.org/thinking-sensing-and-behaving/aging/2019/how-the-brain-changes-with-age-083019
2. Strauch, Barbara. *The secret life of the grown-up brain: The surprising talents of the middle-aged mind* (Viking, 1st edition, 2010).
3. James, Geoffrey. "Neuroscience: Relaxing Makes You More Creative," *Inc.com.* (January 12, 2015) https://www.inc.com/geoffrey-james/neuroscience-relaxing-makes-you-more-creative.html

4. Booth, Stephanie. "How Stress Can Shrink Your Brain and 6 Ways to Keep It from Happening," *Healthline*. (November 21, 2018) https://www.healthline.com/health-news/how-stress-can-shrink-your-brain
5. Sapolsky, Robert M. "Stress and Your Shrinking Brain," *Stanford University*. (1999) https://sites.oxy.edu/clint/physio/article/stressandyourshrinkingbrain.pdf
6. Raichle, Marcus E., and Debra A. Gusnard. "Appraising the brain's energy budget" *Research Gate*. (September 2002). https://www.researchgate.net/publication/11232262_Appraising_the_brain's_energy_budget
https://www.brainfacts.org/thinking-sensing-and-behaving/aging/2019/healthy-aging-091019
7. Mehta, Ravi and Rui Juliet Zhu. "Blue or Red? Exploring the Effect of Color on Cognitive Task Performances," *Urbana-Champaign*, University of Illinois, Cheung Kong Graduate School of Business. (March 2009). https://www.researchgate.net/publication/23983380_Blue_or_Red_Exploring_the_Effect_of_Color_on_Cognitive_Task_Performances
8. Park, Alice. "Why Sunlight Is So Good For You," *Time Magazine*. (August 7, 2017) https://time.com/4888327/why-sunlight-is-so-good-for-you/
9. Laland, Kevin N. "These amazing creative animals show why humans are the most innovative species of all," *The Conversation*. (April 20, 2017) https://theconversation.com/these-amazing-creative-animals-show-why-humans-are-the-most-innovative-species-of-all-75515

Chapter 9

1. Dr. Todd Thatcher. "The top ten benefits of spending time with family". Highland Springs. (March 17, 2020) https://highlandspringsclinic.org/blog/the-top-ten-benefits-of-spending-time-with-family/
2. Sam Paul. "American families barely spend quality time together". New York post. (March 20, 2018) https://nypost.com/2018/03/20/american-families-barely-spend-quality-time-together/
3. Jenny Anderson. "In the age of screens, families are spending more time "alone-together"". Quartz. (March 16, 2019) https://qz.com/1573329/are-families-spending-less-time-together-due-to-screens/
4. Al-Shorachi, Evan, Koonlada Sasasmit, and Milene Goncalves. "Creativity Intervention: Using Storytelling and Math Problemsas Intervening Tasks for Inducing Incubation," *Research Gate*. University of Technology, The Netherlands. (accessed: February 2021) https://www.researchgate.net/publication/280735975_CREATIVITY_INTERVENTION_USING_STORYTELLING_AND_MATH_PROBLEMS_AS_INTERVENING_TASKS_FOR_INDUCING_INCUBATION
5. Sio, Ut Na, and Thomas C. Ormerod. "Does incubation enhance problem-solving? A meta-analytic review," Research *Gate*. (accessed: February 2021) DOI: 10.1037/a0014212
6. Gilhooly, Kenneth J. "Incubation and Intuition in CreativeProblem Solving," *Frontiers*. (July 22, 2016) https://www.frontiersin.org/articles/10.3389/fpsyg.2016.01076/full

Chapter 10

1. Joyce, Caneel K., "The Blank Page: Effects of Constraint on Creativity," *SSRN*. (December 16, 2009) Available at SSRN: https://ssrn.com/abstract=1552835

Chapter 11

1. Barsh, Joanna, Marla M. Capozzi, and Jonathan Davidson. "Leadership and innovation." *Mckinsey* (January 1, 2008). https://www.mckinsey.com/business-functions/strategy-and-corporate-finance/our-insights/leadership-and-innovation
2. "Crowdsourcing Drug Development." Whitepaper, InnoCentive, (accessed: December 28, 2020). https://www.innocentive.com/wp-content/uploads/2019/09/Crowdsourcing_Drug_Development_4.0.pdf

Chapter 12

1. World Health Organisation. "Newborns: improving survival and well-being," *The World Health Organisation Newsroom*. (September 2020) https://www.who.int/news-room/fact-sheets/detail/newborns-reducing-mortality#:~:text=Globally%202.4%20million%20children%20died,in%20child%20survival%20since%201990.
2. Sower, Victor E., Jo Ann Duffy, and Gerald Kohers. "Great Ormond Street Hospital for Children: Ferrari's Formula One Handovers and Handovers from Surgery to Intensive Care," *American Society for Quality*. (August 2008) https://www.gwern.net/docs/technology/2008-sower.pdf

Chapter 14

1. Perry, Mark J. "Fortune 500 firms 1955 v. 2017: Only 60 remain, thanks to the creative destruction that fuels economicprosperity," *AEI*. (October 20, 2017) https://www.aei.org/carpe-diem/fortune-500-firms-1955-v-2017-only-12-remain-thanks-to-the-creative-destruction-that-fuels-economic-prosperity/#:~:text=In%20other%20words%2C%20fewer%20than,Fortune%20500%20companies%20(ranked%20by

Chapter 15

1. Uber. "So, what is Uber all about? Fun facts about the Uber story," *Uber Blog*. (blog). (January 16, 2020) https://www.uber.com/en-QA/blog/facts-about-uber/#:~:text=The%20inspiration%20for%20Uber%20came,has%20been%20growing%20ever%20since
2. OECD. "HM1.3 HOUSING TENURES," OECD—Social Policy Division—Directorate of Employment, Labour and Social Affairs. (updated: May 31, 2021) https://www.oecd.org/els/family/HM1-3-Housing-tenures.pdf
3. "Australia: Number of cars per household," *.id*. (December 2020) https://www.abs.gov.au/statistics/industry/tourism-and-transport/motor-vehicle-census-australia/latest-release

A Little Bit About Me...

I am a passionate educator with a mission to empower teachers and parents to create tomorrow's innovators.

I started my career as a computer scientist and worked for top global hi-tech companies such as IBM and Mercury for several years. Working at the forefront of this cutting-edge industry helped me understand the impact of technology on the future of work.

Additionally, as I watched my three sons' journeys through primary school, I realised they were not being prepared for this future.

While I saw the movement towards STEM as going in the right direction, important skills such as creative thinking and the development of an innovative mindset, to name a few, were being left out. Having a strong technological background and being a Design Thinking practitioner, I was able to see that there was a need and a way to bridge this gap.

Therefore, I co-founded "Glittering Minds" https://www.glitteringminds.com.au/ and designed a programme for schools. This programme creates the needed paradigm shift in education by introducing Design Thinking as the new pedagogy.

I also have a podcast called "The Thinking Effect" to help educators around the globe create great thinkers.

I have been a teacher educator for a few years now. I have been privileged with the opportunity to guide, support, and empower teachers to create a deeper, authentic, innovative, student-centred educational setting in their classrooms. It brings me happiness to see firsthand how participation in Glittering Minds programme transforms both teachers' and students' ways of thinking and creates a learning environment that meets the twenty-first-century needs.

www.ingramcontent.com/pod-product-compliance
Lightning Source LLC
Chambersburg PA
CBHW051423290426
44109CB00016B/1407